History Odyssey

Middle Ages
level two

Kathleen Johnson

 Pandia Press

Important information on Web links:

Web site links are provided to assist students in research. At the time of printing this guide, all Web sites listed were functional. Because Web site content changes frequently, Pandia Press cannot guarantee the availability of Web links provided nor can we be responsible for Internet viruses, or inappropriate, inaccurate, or objectionable materials. We encourage parents and teachers to monitor and supervise students while on the Internet. We highly recommend the use of Internet filtering software and recommend students avoid chat rooms, downloads, and giving personal information while on the Internet. (Please e-mail Web link problems to kate@pandiapress.com.)

Copyright 2006, 2013 Pandia Press
All Rights Reserved
Without limiting the rights under copyright reserved above, no part of this publication may be reproduced, stored in or introduced into a retrieval system, or transmitted in any form by any means (electronic, mechanical, photocopying, recording, or otherwise), without the prior written permission of Pandia Press. The purchaser of this study guide may photocopy maps and worksheets for use with his or her children. Copying for group, co-op, classroom, or school use is prohibited. Contact Pandia Press for information about ordering extra worksheets, and maps, and about school licensing.

ISBN: 978-0-9766057-4-4

Published by
Pandia Press
Mount Dora, FL

Visit www.pandiapress.com for sample pages of Pandia Press publications and for ordering information.

Table of Contents

Letter to Parents and Teachers / How to Use This Guide 4

Part I Europe in the Middle Ages 9

    Lesson 1 Barbarians 11

    Lessons 2 - 3 Monasticism 11

    Lesson 4 *The Door in the Wall* 12

    Lessons 5 - 6 Jewish Persecution 12

    Lessons 7 - 8 Religion in the Middle Ages 13

    Lesson 9 The Carolingians 14

    Lesson 10 Charlemagne 14

    Lesson 11 Central Europe 14

    Lesson 12 *The Trumpeter of Krakow* 15

    Lesson 13 Anglo - Saxon Britain 15

    Lesson 14 *Beowulf, A New Telling* 15

    Lessons 15 - 16 Scotland 16

    Lessons 17 - 21 The Vikings 16

    Lessons 22 - 23 The Normans 18

    Lesson 24 Feudalism 19

    Lesson 25 Knighthood 19

    Lesson 26 Chivalry 19

    Lesson 27 *The Story of King Arthur and his Knights* 19

    Lesson 28 The Holy Roman Empire 20

    Lesson 29 Medieval Art and Inventions 20

    Lesson 30 Illuminated Letter Project 21

    Lesson 31 Capetian France 21

    Lessons 32 - 34 The Crusades 21

    Lesson 35 Henry of Anjou 22

    Lesson 36 *The Adventures of Robin Hood* 23

    Lessons 37 - 38 Charter and Parliament 23

    Lessons 39 - 40 Ireland 24

    Lessons 41 - 42 *Adam of the Road* 24

    Lessons 43 - 45 European Trade 25

    Lessons 46 - 47 Medieval Architecture 26

Table of Contents

Lessons 48 Medieval Explorers	27
Lessons 49 - 50 The Black Death	27
Lessons 51 - 52 The Hundred Years' War	28
Lessons 53 - 54 *The Canterbury Tales*	29

Part II Asia 31

Lesson 55 The Byzantine Empire	33
Lesson 56 Justinian	33
Lessons 57 - 58 Islam and Baghdad	33
Lesson 59 The Seljuk Turks	34
Lesson 60 *One Thousand and One Arabian Nights*	35
Lesson 61 Bulgaria and Kiev	35
Lesson 62 Russia	35
Lesson 63 Constantinople and the End of Byzantium	36
Lesson 64 Safavid Persia	36
Lesson 65 The Ottoman Empire	37
Lesson 66 Sui and Tang China	37
Lesson 67 The Song Dynasty in China	38
Lessons 68 - 69 The Mongols	38
Lesson 70 The Ming Dynasty in China	39
Lesson 71 India	39
Lesson 72 Japan	40
Lesson 73 Fujiwara Japan	40
Lesson 74 Feudalism in Japan	40
Lesson 75 *Tales of the Heike*	41
Lesson 76 Samurai versus Knight	41
Lesson 77 Haiku	42
Lesson 78 Japan and China in the Renaissance	42
Lesson 79 Thailand and Vietnam	43

Part III The Americas 45

Lesson 80 North America	47
Lessons 81 - 82 The Maya	47
Lesson 83 The Aztecs and the Incas	48

Table of Contents

    Lesson 84 The Aztecs 48

    Lesson 85 The Incas 49

    Lesson 86 The Maya, Aztecs, and Incas 49

Part IV Africa 51

    Lesson 87 Ghana, "The Land of Gold" 53

    Lesson 88 Mali and Ethiopia 53

    Lesson 89 Sundiata, The Lion King 54

    Lesson 90 Benin and Zimbabwe 54

    Lesson 91 Songhay 54

Part V Europe in the Renaissance 57

    Lessons 92 - 93 Introduction to the Renaissance 59

    Lesson 94 The Spanish Inquisition 59

    Lesson 95 The Portuguese Empire 60

    Lessons 96 - 98 European Explorers 61

    Lesson 99 The Conquistadors and the Spanish Empire 62

    Lesson 100 The Powerful Hapsburgs 62

    Lesson 101 Dutch Independence 63

    Lesson 102 The Spanish Armada 63

    Lessons 103 - 104 Tudor England 63

    Lessons 105 - 106 France 64

    Lesson 107 The Reformation and Counter-Reformation 65

    Lessons 108 - 109 Italy 65

    Lesson 110 Renaissance Art, Writings, and Inventions 66

    Lesson 111 Shakespeare 66

    Lesson 112 From the Middle Ages to the Renaissance 66

    Lesson 113 Timeline Analysis 67

Appendix A How to Write a Biography and Attribution of Sources 69

Appendix B The Magna Carta 72

Appendix C Plot Diagram 77

Appendix D "Sundiata, The Lion King of Mali" 79

Appendix E Recommended Resources 90

Attachments: Worksheets
                      Maps

Dear Parents and Teachers,

Your child is about to embark on a great adventure—studying the history of humankind. History Odyssey guides are intended to assist your child on this adventure with access to the greatest resources and with assistance in organizing a tremendous amount of information. This guide is written for the logic- to rhetoric-stage of a classical education (approximately sixth to tenth grade) and will challenge your child to compare and contrast, analyze, research, write, and outline. This study guide expands upon the skills taught in History Odyssey Ancients (level two). Specifically, this guide contains lessons about creating detailed outlines, biographies, and several literary concepts and activities. Students who did not complete Ancients (level two), should be able to successfully complete this course if they have some prior knowledge of basic outlining and summarizing.

This study guide contains many writing assignments. Although basic instructions are given, History Odyssey is not a writing course. I highly recommend that students complete a formal writing class prior to or during this course.

In order to eliminate confusion, history in this guide is (for the most part) presented chronologically by region. The course begins with a study of the Middle Ages in Europe and ends with a study of the Renaissance in Europe. In between is a non-European study of the Middle Ages and the Renaissance in other parts of the world. At the end of this study guide is the Timeline Analysis that will assist your student in looking back at events chronologically and further analyzing those which were occurring simultaneously in different parts of the world.

The lesson plans in this study guide speak directly to your student for independent use. However, I recommend assisting with the first few lessons and acknowledge that some students may need assistance throughout the course. Read over the following instruction pages with your child and assist him or her in setting up a binder and gathering resources. Most of the lessons are written to be completed in one to two sittings. The exceptions to this are the lessons that instruct students to read one of the eleven literature books, those containing an essay assignment, and those requiring extended research. For these lessons, students should be given ample time to complete the tasks before going on to the next lesson unless otherwise indicated. If your child's interest is sparked by a subject, refer to the resource list and allow him or her to spend extra time on that subject. I suggest students at this grade level spend about two hours studying history three to four days a week. At that pace, this guide provides a one-year history course. Keep in mind that these lesson plans combine several subjects—history, literature, writing, and geography.

Most of the literature books used in this study guide are at a level that logic stage students can read independently. Some students may benefit from having the books read aloud. Students will not be interrupted with comprehension questions or vocabulary work while reading the assigned literature. I feel that interrupting the reading of these wonderful books tends to make reading laborious and frustrating. However, you might want to suggest that your child read with a pencil in hand and circle difficult words to look up later. Also, it is recommended that you have discussions with your child during the reading to ensure comprehension. Ideally, you will read the books as well.

There are references to Web sites throughout this study guide. All Web site references provide optional resources for research. I highly recommend students not use the Internet exclusively for their research. In today's high-tech world, it is easy for students to engage in "lazy research" by depending solely on the Internet for information. Although the Internet does contain valuable information, it also contains vast amounts of inaccurate information and harmful materials (see our disclaimer about Web sites on the copyright page). Please guide and supervise your child in Internet research and encourage him to engage in plenty of "old fashioned" library research as well.

How To Use This Guide

Required Resources

The following resources are required to complete this course. Optional resources and book suggestions can be found in the appendix.

*These resources will be used for several years in all level two History Odyssey study guides.

- ☐ *The Kingfisher History Encyclopedia* (1999 or later edition) - KFH
- ☐ **The Story of Mankind* by Hendrik Willem Van Loon (optional) - TSOM †
- ☐ **The History Odyssey Timeline* from Pandia Press (or a homemade timeline)
- ☐ *The Usborne Internet - Linked Viking World* ††
- ☐ *One Thousand and One Arabian Nights* retold by Geraldine McCaughrean
- ☐ *The Door in the Wall* by Marguerite de Angeli
- ☐ *Tales from Shakespeare* by Charles and Mary Lamb
- ☐ *A Shakespeare Coloring Book* from Bellerophon Books **
- ☐ *Beowulf, A New Telling* by Robert Nye
- ☐ *The Story of King Arthur and His Knights* by Howard Pyle
- ☐ *The Adventures of Robin Hood* by Roger Lancelyn Green
- ☐ *Castle* by David Macaulay
- ☐ *Adam of the Road* by Elizabeth Janet Gray
- ☐ *The Canterbury Tales* by Geoffrey Chaucer, retold by Geraldine McCaughrean
- ☐ *Tales from Japan* retold by Helen & William McAlpine
- ☐ *The Trumpeter of Krakow* by Eric P. Kelly

† *The Story of Mankind*: Due to the polarizing nature of *The Story of Mankind* by Hendrick Van Loon, it is optional reading in this level two course. It should be considered a possible resource for gathering information. If students choose not to read TSOM, they might need to seek out other resources to complete some of the lessons. There is a free eBook edition of TSOM available at: *www.gutenberg.org/ebooks/754*

†† In 2008, *Viking World* went out of print in the United States, but might still be available to many customers in the UK, and to all via online bookstores. For those unable to obtain a copy, website references have been added to the lessons with assignments from this book. Alternatively, *The Penguin Historical Atlas of the Vikings* by John Haywood is a High School-level substitute for *Viking World*.

** Bellerophon Books has given permission for students to copy pages from *A Shakespeare Coloring Book* to create their Shakespeare book as instructed in this guide.

Other Supplies Needed

- Three-ring binder (2-inch size is recommended)
- Seven binder dividers with tabs
- Lined paper or computer paper
- A three-hole punch
- A detailed atlas or world wall map
- A ruler or straight edge
- Colored pencils
- Markers, paint pens, and/or paint
- Internet access
- Dictionary, encyclopedias, and library access
- Gold leaf (optional)

Setting Up Your Binder

Divide your binder into the following seven sections:

1. Summaries
2. Men & Women
3. Wars & Conflicts
4. Religion & Mythology
5. Art, Inventions, & Architecture
6. Maps & Worksheets
7. Timeline

Insert this study guide in the front of your binder. Label the dividers and insert lined paper into the first five sections. Three-hole-punch your timeline* and place it along with the maps and worksheets in their appropriate sections.

*Alternatively, you can display your timeline on a wall while you are working on it, and then place it in your binder when finished. See the next page for information on making your own timeline.

How to Use This Guide

Lesson Assignments

Throughout these lessons you will be asked to summarize readings by finding central ideas and outlining. You will also mark dates on your timeline, color and label maps, and read from the list of resources. Try to do all of the assignments listed. When asked to add a person or event to your binder, title your entry and include some important information. Place the entry in the appropriate section of your binder. A short summary is one to two sentences. A lengthy summary should be a complete paragraph consisting of at least five sentences. When you are finished with this course you will have a binder full of information you have learned and work you have completed. More importantly, you will have an education about middle ages history to treasure always.

Map Work

Geography is an important part of history and you will be learning a great deal of geography throughout this course. When working with a map, carefully color areas with colored pencils. Do not use markers, as they will bleed through the paper and blot out labels and other markings. You can make the land areas colorful by coloring each country or area a different pastel shade. When labeling, use a ruler to lightly make a pencil line. Print the name carefully on the line with a fine-point black pen and then erase the pencil line after your ink dries. Take your time to make the maps beautiful keepsake treasures of your time spent studying middle ages history.

Outlining

In this course, you will be taught advanced outlining, then asked to outline certain readings from *Kingfisher History Encyclopedia*. Outlining is a very important skill to learn. If you learn this skill well it will help you tremendously when reading complicated writings, when preparing notes for oral presentations and research papers, and when taking notes in high school and college courses. Outlining will help you separate main ideas from details. It will help you break down information into the most important parts and organize them.

Timeline

You will need a timeline to complete this course. Using a timeline will assist you in organizing information and seeing connections between events. At the end of this course, you will be completing an interesting exercise in which you analyze the data on your timeline. Timelines can be purchased or constructed. To construct your own timeline you will need a piece of butcher paper about 3½ feet long. Draw a line across the paper a few inches from the top. Leaving a little space at the beginning of your line for earlier events, mark dates beginning at the year 400 AD. Continue marking dates in 50-year increments ending with the year 1700. Space your dates approximately 3 inches apart. Accordion-fold the timeline, three-hole-punch it, and place it in your binder.

How to Use This Guide

As you enter events on the timeline you can either draw lines from the information to the point they occurred on the timeline, or you can enter a reference number on the timeline that refers to a corresponding entry on a separate piece of paper. (See examples of these two methods below.)

Note: In this course, dates are indicated as BC (before Christ) and AD (anno Domini) because these are the traditional abbreviations that are used in KFH, TSOM, and other books in utilized in this course. You should also be aware of the secular abbreviations used in some modern books. These are BCE (before common era), used instead of BC, and CE (common era), used instead of AD.

Write events directly on your timeline:

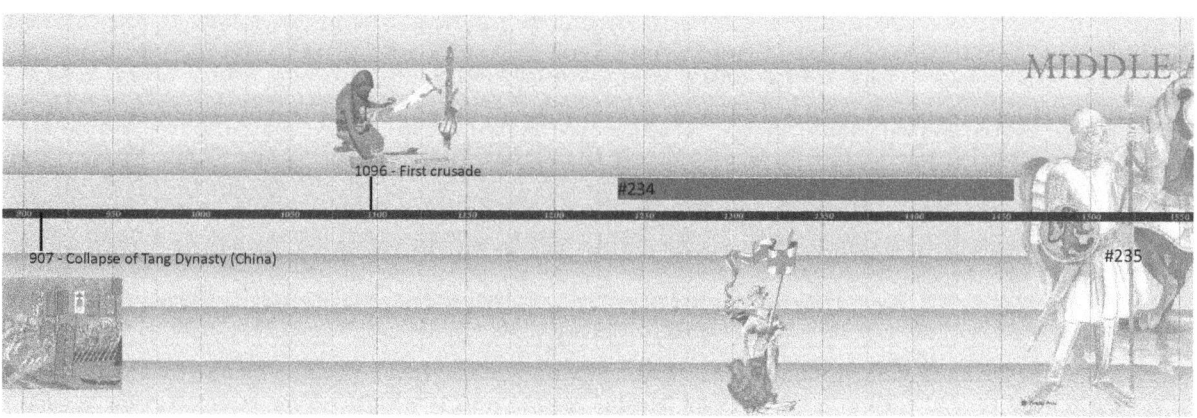

Write reference numbers on your timeline that refer to entries on separate paper:

#234 -
1337 to 1453 Hundred Year's War. England vs. France. Began when Edward II claimed the French throne. England won only Calais and Channel islands in the end.

#235 –
1519 to 1521 Spanish invasion of Mexico. Conquistador, Hernando Cortés, conquered Mexico in search of gold and silver.

Part I
Europe in the Middle Ages

Lesson 1: Barbarians

GET READY For this lesson you will need:

- KFH
- Map 1: Barbarian Invasion
- TSOM (optional)
- Fine-point black pen or pencil
- Colored pencils
- Atlas

If you studied ancient history last year, you know about the barbarian invasion and the Fall of Rome. This lesson is a quick review of geography and the end of ancient history.

☐ Read KFH pp. 82 - 83, The Barbarians.

☐ Read TSOM Chapter 26, The Fall of Rome.

☐ On map 1, color each continent a different color. There are sections of three different continents shown on this map. Use an atlas and the map on p. 99 of KFH to assist you in identification. (The Middle East is part of the continent of Asia.)

Label the following bodies of water:

Mediterranean Sea	Caspian Sea
Aegean Sea	Black Sea
Atlantic Ocean	

Label the following countries:

Italy	France
Spain	Denmark
Britain	Norway
Ireland	Sweden
Greece	
Hungary	

You may choose to label other countries that you find on your modern day atlas. See if you can remember where Athens, Constantinople, Carthage, and Rome are located. Label them on your map with a dot. (A dot is the proper way to identify a city or town on a map.)

Lesson 2: Monasticism

GET READY For this lesson you will need:

- KFH
- Timeline

☐ Read KFH pp. 102-103, Monasticism.

☐ In the Religion & Mythology section of your binder, list the duties and events that took place in monasteries. Don't forget to title your work.

☐ Also in your Religion & Mythology section, write a short summary of each of the following people:

St. Benedict	**St. Francis of Assisi**
St. Dominic	**Venerable Bede**

☐ Record significant dates on your timeline:

- 269   1st monastery (Egypt)
- 540   St. Benedict writes Benedictine rule
- 731   Venerable Bede writes "The Ecclesiastical History of the English People"
- 1054   Great Schism (split of the Roman Catholic and Orthodox church)

☐ Summarize the following monastic orders in your Religion & Mythology section:

Benedictines	**Cluniacs**
Cistercians	**Dominicans**
Franciscans	

Lesson 3: Monasticism (cont.)

GET READY For this lesson you will need:

- Drawing paper, colored pencils, art supplies
- *The Door in the Wall*

☐ Draw a detailed floor plan of a monastery from a bird's eye view. Be creative, label the different buildings, draw people and livestock. Add color to your drawing and give your monastery village a name. Place your drawing in your Religion & Mythology section. While working on your drawing, you may proceed with the next lesson and begin reading *The Door in the Wall*.

 ## Lesson 4: The Door in the Wall

GET READY For this lesson you will need:

- *The Door in the Wall*

❑ Read *The Door in the Wall* by Marguerite de Angeli. Try to read this short, enjoyable book in one week or less. This book takes place in England during the reign of Edward III of whom you will soon learn more. It portrays life in a monastery and demonstrates how a monastery assisted its community.

❑ When you finish reading *The Door in the Wall*, complete this writing assignment: Summarize your answers to the following questions and place in your Summaries section.

What did Brother Luke mean when he said "reading is a door in the wall" and "thou haste only to follow the wall far enough and there will be a door in it"?

Can you think of a talent or skill that you have that could be a door in the wall?

How could your talents open doors for you?

 ## Lesson 5: Jewish Persecution

GET READY For this lesson you will need:

- KFH
- Dictionary

❑ Read KFH pp. 108-109, Persecution of Jews.

❑ Outline these pages by creating main topics and subtopics. Title your outline "Persecution of the Jews and Diaspora" and place it in your Summaries section. Remember what you learned about outlining in the ancient history course. Suggested main topic sentences for your outline:

I. The Jews of Judea fought against their Roman rulers.

II. Christian Romans became increasingly intolerant.

III. In Europe, anti-Semitism spread and Jews did not have the same rights as Christians.

IV. During the Crusades, feelings towards Jews hardened even more.

You may use these or create your own. Add at least two subtopics under each main topic. (Remember that subtopics are listed A, B, C, etc. under each main topic.)

❑ Look up the following in a dictionary and write the definitions in your Religion & Mythology section:

Semite	**Yiddish**
Anti-Semitism	**Rabbi**
Torah	

Diaspora (If not in your dictionary, use the definition found in KFH.)

 ## Lesson 6: Jewish Persecution (cont.)

GET READY For this lesson you will need:
- KFH
- Map 2: The Diaspora
- Colored pencils
- Drawing paper, ruler, scissors, tape
- Paperclip

❑ Throughout history and even today, Jewish people are sometimes unfairly associated with money or being miserly. Describe in a paragraph how this prejudice and other forms of anti-Semitism began in the Middle Ages. (Information can be found in your reading of KFH during the last lesson.) Title your work "Anti-Semitism" and place it in your Summaries or Religion & Mythology section.

❑ On map 2, color land areas. Referring to the map in KFH on p. 108, label countries, cities, and water areas. Trace in red the routes of the Diaspora from Jerusalem and from Rome. Notice that some Jews moved into Spain which was under Islamic rule. The Islamic Kingdom was tolerant of the Jewish people in the Middle Ages.

- Create a mini-timeline on Diaspora in your Religion & Mythology section. Cut a strip of paper 11 inches by 3 inches. Draw a horizontal line down the center. At the left end of the line mark the date 1 AD, and at the other end mark 1400. Mark the dates in between at 50-year increments (the middle should lie at 700). Accordion-fold the strip so that when folded the outside square is blank. (To make a neat accordion-fold, fold the timeline in half then in half again. Use the crease lines to refold the timeline accordion-style.) Write "Diaspora" on the outside square and glue or tape the left end to a piece of paper in your Religion & Mythology section. A paperclip will help hold your timeline closed. Begin marking your timeline at 70 AD (when the Jews were barred from entering Jerusalem), and end in 1306 (when Jews were expelled from France). Remember to record the dates on your main timeline as well. You may want to add drawings to your mini-timeline to make it colorful.

Religion in the Middle Ages (cont.)

GET READY For this lesson you will need:
- Library access
- Appendix A: How to Write a Biography and Attribution of Sources
- Appendix E: Recommended Resources

- Read Appendix A: How to Write a Biography and Attribution of Sources.

- Library trip! Research at least one of the religious leaders (listed below) from the Middle Ages and write a biography. Place your work in your Religion & Mythology section. Instructions on writing on a biography can be found in Appendix A. Include a bibliography at the end of your biography. In the bibliography, list the books that you used to research your report. Refer to Appendix A for instruction on how to properly attribute a source. Place your biography in your Men & Women section.

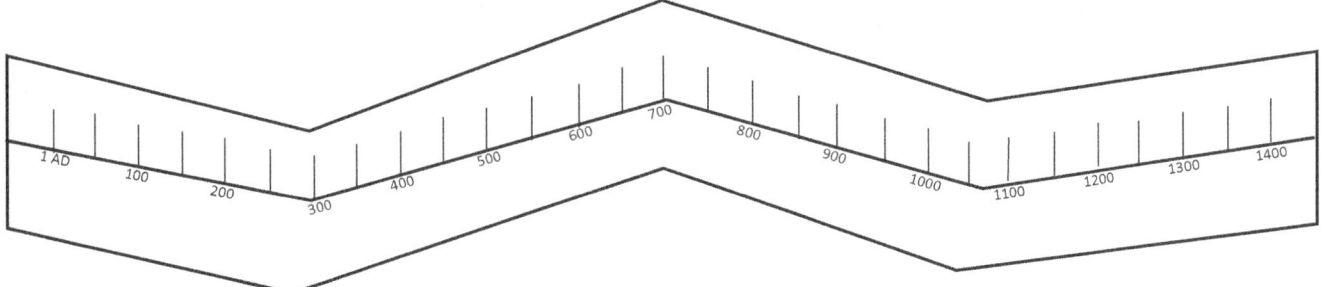

Religion in the Middle Ages

GET READY For this lesson you will need:
- KFH

- Read KFH pp. 168 - 169, Religion in the Middle Ages.

- In the Religion & Mythology section of your binder, write detailed summaries about the different religions during the Middle Ages. Include the religious beliefs of Christians, Muslims, Hindus, Buddhists, and the Maya. Add information on Judaism from prior lessons. Include which part of the world the religion was practiced and other interesting facts.

Religious leaders from the middle ages:

Meister Eckhart

Ibn Arabi

Thomas Aquinas

Maimonides

Ramanuja

Dogen

St. Francis of Assisi

Marpa the Translator

Lesson 9: The Carolingians

GET READY For this lesson you will need:
- KFH
- TSOM (optional)
- Timeline
- Map 3: The Empire of Charlemagne

☐ Read KFH pp. 114 - 115, The Carolingians.

☐ Outline these pages and title it "The Carolingians." Include main topics and subtopics. Place this outline in your Summaries section.

☐ Read TSOM Chapter 29, Charlemagne (also covers Otto I who will be studied again in a future lesson).

☐ Add the following to your Men & Women section along with short summaries of each:

the Franks

Clovis

Charles Martel

Roland (You might read "The Song of Roland" in high school.)

Pepin

Charlemagne (leave room to add more later)

☐ Record significant dates on your timeline:

- 486   France united by Clovis
- 751   Pepin, the first Carolingian king
- 768   Charlemagne becomes Carolingian king
- 782   Charlemagne defeats the Saxons
- 800   Pope Leo III crowns Charlemagne Roman Emperor
- 814   Charlemagne dies
- 843   Carolingian Empire divided into three parts

☐ On map 3, shade the empire controlled by Charlemagne in 870 (outlined in black). Label the different regions as indicated on p. 114 in KFH. Label the islands to the north of the empire. Label France, the Pyrenees Mountains, the Atlantic Ocean, the Mediterranean Sea, and Spain. Label the cities of Rome, Aachen, Poitiers, and Tours (with a dot).

Lesson 10: Charlemagne

GET READY For this lesson you will need:
- Library access

☐ Library trip! Research Charlemagne. Write a biography of his life and accomplishments. Place your biography of Charlemagne in your Men & Women section.

Lesson 11: Central Europe

GET READY For this lesson you will need:
- KFH
- Map 4: Medieval Europe
- Atlas
- Timeline

☐ Read KFH pp. 120 - 121, Magyars and Bohemians.

☐ Outline this reading and title it "Magyars and Bohemians." Include main topics and subtopics. Place this outline in your Summaries section.

☐ On map 4, label Bohemia, Bulgaria, Moravia, and Poland. Also label the Mediterranean Sea, the Black Sea, the Baltic sea, the North Sea, and the Atlantic Ocean. Refer to the map in KFH p. 120 and your atlas while labeling. Label four other countries, Constantinople, Kiev, and Novgorod. Locate Krakow, Poland in your atlas and label it on your map. Locate the Czech Republic in your atlas and label in parentheses under Bohemia and Moravia on your map. In your modern day atlas, find Kazakhstan.

☐ Add the following to your Men & Women section: **Prince Arpad**
    Duke ("good king") Wenceslas

☐ Record significant dates on your timeline:

- 920   Wenceslas tries to modernize Bohemia
- 960   Unification of Poland
- 1241 Collapse of Hungary after Mongol raid
- 1260 Peak of Bohemian power
- 1380 Bohemia and Moravia under German control

- Optional: Read the lyrics and listen to the Christmas carol titled "Good King Wenceslas." You can listen at this website - www.carols.org.uk/good_king_wenceslas.htm

Lesson 12: The Trumpeter of Krakow

GET READY For this lesson you will need:
- *The Trumpeter of Krakow*

- Read *The Trumpeter of Krakow* by Eric P. Kelly in one to two weeks. This fictional story takes place in Poland during the Middle Ages when Kiev in Russia was founded by the Viking Ros leader, Rurik. The "Tartars" mentioned in the story refer to the cruel Mongols who invaded Russia and China in the 13th, 14th, and 15th centuries. You will learn about the Vikings, Kiev, and the Mongols in future lessons.

Lesson 13: Anglo-Saxon Britain

GET READY For this lesson you will need:
- KFH
- Timeline

- Read KFH pp. 122 - 123, Anglo-Saxon Britain.

- Outline this reading. This time when outlining, include more information by adding details to your sub-topics. The details are numbered 1, 2, 3, etc. in your outline and indented under A, B, C, etc. Title your outline and place it in your Summaries section. Your outline could begin like this:

I. After the Romans left Britain, there was a struggle for power.
   A. The Saxons from Germany were invited into Britain as mercenaries but quickly started to conquer land.
      1. They gained control of the southeast.
      2. The legendary King Arthur held them back for awhile.
      3. In 552 they started taking over southern and central England.
   B. Many Britons were negatively affected.
      1. Many were killed.
      2. Many lost land and immigrated to other parts of Europe.

II. Many Germans emigrated to Britain creating the birth of England
(write at least two subtopics and include details)

III. United England experienced new power struggles.
(write at least two subtopics and include details)

- Record significant dates on your timeline:

  560   Saxons begin to invade Britain
  597   The Pope sends Augustine to convert the Saxons
  793   The first Viking raid on England
  871   Alfred the Great crowned king of Wessex
  1013 Danes conquer England
  1066 Normans conquer England

- Add the following to your Men & Women section along with a short summary:

  St. Augustine
  King Canute (the Great)
  Duke William
  King Arthur
  Alfred the Great

Lesson 14: Beowulf, A New Telling

GET READY For this lesson you will need:
- *Beowulf, A New Telling*
- Worksheet: Elements of an Epic

- Read *Beowulf, A New Telling* by Robert Nye. This epic story was written by an unknown author during the Middle Ages in Anglo-Saxon England. When you have finished reading *Beowulf*, complete the following writing assignment:

- *Beowulf* is considered an epic. An epic is a narrative poem which celebrates the deeds of a legendary superhero or god. The *Iliad* and the *Odyssey* are also considered epic poetry. Some modern-day epic stories include *Star Wars*, *Harry Potter*, the *Narnia* series, and *The Lord of the Rings*. Why does *Beowulf* qualify as an epic? To find out, complete the Elements of an Epic worksheet. After you complete the worksheet, summarize in one or two paragraphs why *Beowulf* is an epic. Place the worksheet and your summary in the Summaries section of your binder.

 ## Scotland

GET READY For this lesson you will need:
- *Viking World*
- *Tales from Shakespeare*
- Atlas

Although William Shakespeare was not born until 1564, you will be reading his plays when studying the regions of their settings. As you read Shakespeare, you will be constructing a Shakespeare book consisting of summaries from your reading and coloring pages from your Shakespeare coloring book.

❑ At the time of Macbeth, Scotland had undergone years of raids and settlement by the Vikings. Refer to p. 34 of *Viking World* for a map of Scotland, Wales, and Ireland. On a modern-day map or atlas locate this area. Scotland, England, Wales, and Ireland are often referred to as the British Isles. Scotland, England, and Wales make up Great Britain, and together along with Northern Ireland, they form the United Kingdom.

❑ Read "Macbeth" starting on p. 152 in *Tales from Shakespeare* by Charles and Mary Lamb. When you have finished, refer to the next lesson for an assignment.

 ## Scotland (cont.)

GET READY For this lesson you will need:
- *Tales from Shakespeare*
- *A Shakespeare Coloring Book*
- Colored pencils

Duncan was an actual king of Scotland during the Middle Ages whose reputation was much improved by Shakespeare. In reality, Duncan was not meek but rather vicious and inclined to war. He invaded northern England several times. He also tried many times to slay Macbeth before Macbeth killed him in 1040 and himself became king of Scotland. Macbeth has been described as a good king. In Irish records he has been described as "the ruddy-complexioned, yellow-haired tall one in whom I shall rejoice." In 1057, Macbeth was slain by a son of Duncan.

Macbeth is considered one of Shakespeare's darkest plays. He wrote *Macbeth* in the 17th century to be performed for King James I of England (also known as James IV of Scotland). King James apparently believed in the supernatural and witchcraft. Shakespeare reportedly wrote the play to please him.

❑ Today you will create the first pages of what will become your book of Shakespeare. In two or three pages, retell the story of *Macbeth* in your own words. Be detailed and include all of the characters. Copy and then color one or more of the three scenes from *Macbeth* found in your Shakespeare coloring book on pp. 24 - 27. Save your story of *Macbeth* and the coloring pages to create a Shakespeare book later.

 ## The Vikings

GET READY For this lesson you will need:
- KFH
- *Viking World*
- Drawing paper, ruler, scissors, tape
- Paperclip

❑ Read KFH pp. 130 - 131, The Vikings.

❑ Outline this reading and title your outline "The Vikings." Remember to include main topics, subtopics, and details. Place your outline in the Summaries section of your binder.

❑ Read the Introduction, "Who were the Vikings?," and "The age of kings" in *Viking World*. These readings reveal the savage nature of some Scandinavian kings. Would you have liked to have been a king in Scandinavia during the time of the Vikings? You would probably have to watch your back!

Alternatively, visit these Web sites:
www.bbc.co.uk/schools/vikings/invasion/index.shtml
www.jorvik-viking-centre.co.uk/vikings1.htm
www.viking.no/e/people/e-knud.htm - information about the Viking king, Knut

- ☐ Optional: Record the succession of Scandinavian kings in your Men & Women section.

- ☐ Begin a mini timeline on the Vikings. Cut a strip of paper 11 inches by 3 inches. Draw a line down the center. At the left end of the line mark the date 700 and at the other end mark the date 1100. Mark the dates in between at 50 year increments (the year 900 should be in the middle). Accordion-fold the strip so that when folded, the outside square is blank. (To make a neat accordion fold, fold the timeline in half then in half again. Use the crease lines to refold the timeline accordion-style.) Write "Viking Timeline" on the outside square and glue or tape the left end to a piece of paper in your Summaries section. A paperclip will help keep your timeline closed. As you study the Vikings, record dates on your mini-timeline. Remember to record the dates on your main timeline as well. A Viking timeline can be found at www.bbc.co.uk/schools/vikings/timeline.shtml

The Vikings (cont.)

GET READY For this lesson you will need:
- Map 5: The Viking World
- *Viking World*
- Atlas

- ☐ On map 5, label and color the countries of Norway, Sweden, Ireland, England, Iceland, Greenland, Newfoundland, Russia, and Denmark. (Look at a modern day map to find the borders of these countries.) Circle Norway, Sweden, and Denmark and label them "Scandinavia." Using the map on pp. 54 - 55 of *Viking World*, label the cities of Novgorod, Kiev, and Constantinople. Draw a black arrow from Denmark to Iceland to Greenland to Newfoundland. Complete the Map Key by identifying the black arrow as "Viking Expansion."

If *Viking World* is unavailable, use these Web sites for map references:
www.bbc.co.uk/schools/vikings/invasion/index.shtml
en.wikipedia.org/wiki/Image:Vikings-Voyages.png

- ☐ Summarize the reasons why the Vikings began raiding nearby lands. Title your summary and place it in your Wars & Conflicts section.

- ☐ Define *fjord* and describe why you feel the Vikings would want to live on or near a fjord. Place your summary in your Wars & Conflicts section.

The Vikings (cont.)

GET READY For this lesson you will need:
- *Viking World*

- ☐ Read "Life on a Viking farm," "Inside a Viking house," "What the Vikings wore," "Norse woman," "Viking towns," and "Viking society and government" from *Viking World*.

Alternatively, visit these Web sites:
www.regia.org/village.htm
www.pbs.org/wgbh/nova/vikings/village.html#thumb5
www.bbc.co.uk/history/ancient/vikings/launch_vt_viking_farm.shtml
www.yorkarchaeology.co.uk/piclib/photos.php (click on JORVIK and Viking York on the side bar)
www.regia.org/viking2.htm - Viking thralls (slaves)

- ☐ Write a summary titled "How the Vikings Lived." Include information on Viking food, housing, clothing, professions, marriage, families, communities, and government. Your summary should be 1 - 2 pages long. Place your work in the Summaries section of your binder.

The Vikings (cont.)

GET READY For this lesson you will need:
- *Viking World*
- Map 5: The Viking World
- Colored pencils
- Your Viking mini-timeline

- ☐ Read "Viking ships," "Viking warriors," "The raiding begins," "Exploring the northern seas," and "Mainland Europe under attack" from *Viking World*.

Alternatively, visit these websites:

www.hurstwic.org/history/articles/manufacturing/text/norse_ships.htm - Viking ships

www.legendsandchronicles.com/ancient-warriors/viking-warriors/ - Viking warriors

www.bbc.co.uk/history/ancient/vikings/launch_gms_viking_quest.shtml - Viking warrior game

www.mnh.si.edu/vikings/start.html - click on Viking Voyage

- [ ] Add to your Viking mini-timeline.

- [ ] > On map #5 again, use pp. 54 - 55 in *Viking World* as a reference and label water areas. Label Italy, Sicily, France, and Spain. Draw the Viking routes with red arrows on your map. Add to the map key by identifying the routes of the Vikings.

If *Viking World* isn't available, use this pdf for a map reference: www.rmg.co.uk/upload/pdf/Viking_routes.pdf

- [ ] Add the following to your Men & Women section along with a short summary:

   Alfred the Great

   Harald Hardrada "The Last Viking"

   Charlemagne (add to your former entry)

   King Cnut

   Rollo

Lesson 21: The Vikings (cont.)

GET READY For this lesson you will need:

- *Viking World*

- [ ] Read "Death and burial in Viking times," "Norse gods and goddesses," "Christianity during the Viking Age," and "Norse legends" from *Viking World*. Alternatively, visit these websites:

www.hurstwic.org/history/articles/mythology/myths/text/myths.htm - Viking gods

www.bbc.co.uk/history/ancient/vikings/religion_01.shtml - Viking religion

www.lore-and-saga.co.uk/html/viking_burials.html - Viking burials

- [ ] Write a summary titled "Viking Religion." Summarize your readings in this essay including Viking burial rituals, gods, goddesses, worship, and Christianity. Place your summary in your Religion & Mythology section.

Lesson 22: The Normans

GET READY For this lesson you will need:

- KFH
- Map 6: Norman Invasion
- TSOM (optional)
- *Viking World*
- Atlas
- Colored pencils
- Timeline

After the Norman invasion of England in 1066 (The Battle of Hasting), William of Normandy crowned himself king and became William the Conqueror.

- [ ] Read KFH pp. 132 - 133, The Normans.

- [ ] Outline this reading. Include details in your outline.

- [ ] Read TSOM Chapter 30, The Norsemen.

- [ ] Read "The last Viking expeditions" in *Viking World* or visit www.regia.org/norm1.htm

- [ ] > Locate map 6. Using the map on p. 132 of KFH as a reference, label Wales, England, France, London, and Paris. Label water areas. Shade and label the area of Normandy conquered by the Normans under William I. Use your atlas to locate and label Ireland, Scotland, and the English Channel.

- [ ] Add the *Domesday Book* and the Bayeux Tapestry to your Art, Inventions, & Architecture section. (You can read the Bayeux Tapestry scene by scene at www.bayeuxtapestry.org.uk/index.htm)

- [ ] Add significant dates to your timeline.

The Normans (cont.)

GET READY For this lesson you will need:
- Library access

☐ Library Trip! Do research on William the Conqueror and write a biography. Include information on the Battle of Hastings. Include a bibliography of the resources you used and place your report in the Men & Women section of your binder. Place information about the Battle of Hastings in your Wars & Conflicts section.

You can also find information on the Normans and William at *www.bbc.co.uk/history/british/normans/*. If you use information found on a website for your report, you need to include the site in your bibliography.

Feudalism

GET READY For this lesson you will need:
- TSOM (optional)
- Worksheet: Feudalism Chart

☐ Read TSOM Chapter 31, Feudalism.

Feudalism was introduced by William the Conqueror to keep order in Medieval society. At the top of the ladder was the king, then the baron (or lord), then the knight, and finally the serf (also called the villein). The serfs provided food and service, the knight provided protection, the baron provided money and knights to the king. Each in turn granted land to the level below them.

☐ Locate the Feudalism Chart worksheet. This chart maps the hierarchy of the feudal system. Fill in each block on the chart beginning with the king and ending with the serf. Along the arrows, write what each person provided to the level above them and what each received. At the bottom of the worksheet, summarize how feudalism began and what you feel were the benefits and disadvantages. Place the chart in your Summaries section.

Knighthood

GET READY For this lesson you will need:
- KFH

☐ Read KFH pp. 150 - 151, Knighthood.

☐ Summarize the process of becoming a knight. Title your work and place it in the Summaries section of your binder. If you have access to the internet, go to this site for more information for your summary:

library.thinkquest.org/10949/fief/medknight.html

Chivalry

GET READY For this lesson you will need:
- TSOM (optional)

☐ Read TSOM Chapter 32, Chivalry.

☐ Summarize the Code of Chivalry. Also add to the summary you completed in the last lesson by summarizing why knighthood eventually became insignificant and how it finally ended. For more information on chivalry see this website:

www.middle-ages.org.uk/knights-code-of-chivalry.htm

King Arthur and His Knights

GET READY For this lesson you will need:
- *The Story of King Arthur and His Knights*

☐ Read *The Story of King Arthur and His Knights* by Howard Pyle. King Arthur was a legendary hero who may have been based on an actual man who lived during the time of Britain's struggle with the Saxons and Picts. There is no writing assignment for this book; so continue with your lessons while reading *King Arthur*. But try to finish the book before Lesson 36, where you will begin reading another book.

It may take some time to get used to the exaggerated, flowery, and superfluous old English style found in *King Arthur*. But once you do, this book is a lot of fun! You

may even find yourself driving your family crazy by speaking like King Arthur:

"Mother, with great cheerfulness of spirit, I have completed my history work of such greatness that hath never before been seen. And lo! yonder art my companions! I shalt don my jacket in search of adventure and return noon-tide as thou requestith."

The Holy Roman Empire

GET READY For this lesson you will need:
- KFH
- TSOM (optional)
- Map 7: The Holy Roman Empire
- Colored pencils
- Timeline
- Encyclopedia/Internet

☐ Read KFH pp. 124 - 125, The Holy Roman Empire.

☐ Outline these pages and title your outline "The Holy Roman Empire." Place your outline in the Summaries section of your binder.

☐ Read TSOM Chapter 33, Pope vs. Emperor.

☐
> On map 7, shade and label the area controlled by the Empire as indicated on page 124 of KFH. Label the following on your map:
>
> | | |
> |---|---|
> | Britain | Italy |
> | Germany | Hungary |
> | Spain | France |
> | Adriatic Sea | Milan |
> | Atlantic Ocean | Mediterranean Sea |

☐ Record significant dates on your timeline:
- 962   Otto I crowned 1st Holy Roman Emperor in Germany
- 1122   Concordat of Worms bt. Pope and Emperor
- 1200   Peak power of the Catholic Church
- 1300   Pope loses political power

☐ Add the following to your Men & Women section along with a summary of each:
- **Otto the Great (Otto I)**
- **Pope Gregory VII**
- **Henry IV (Germany)**
- **Barbarossa (Red Beard)**
- **Frederick II**
- **Rudolph Hapsburg**

☐ Look up *excommunication* and write a definition in your Religion & Mythology section. Explain why excommunication was such an important and powerful tool of the Church.

Medieval Art and Inventions

GET READY For this lesson you will need:
- KFH
- Timeline
- Worksheet: The Middle Ages Around the World
- Colored pencils

☐ Read KFH:
pp. 138 - 139, The Arts 501 - 1100
pp. 142 - 142, Science and Technology 501 - 1100
pp. 186 - 187, The Arts 1101 - 1460
pp. 190 - 191, Science and Technology 1101 - 1460

☐ Write one summary paragraph each for "The Arts" and "Science and Technology" in the Middle Ages. Place your summary paragraphs in your Art, Inventions, & Architecture section.

☐ Mark dates of major discoveries on your timeline.

☐ Locate the worksheet titled "The Middle Ages Around the World." In each box on the map, list the art, inventions, scientists, and writings that occurred during the Middle Ages in that region of the world. Be sure to include names of the inventors, artists, and writers too. Use information from the readings in this lesson and other lessons. Draw a line from each box to its appropriate place on the map. Color the map and place it in your Art, Inventions, & Architecture section.

❏ Add all of the inventors, scientists, artists, and writers to your Men & Women section that you have not written about previously.

Illuminated Letter Project

GET READY For this lesson you will need:
- Parchment or drawing paper
- Drawing and painting supplies, e.g., paint pens, paint, markers, gold leaf, etc.

Often when monks created books, the first capital letter of each section was written very large and fancy and decorated with real gold and lead. Sometimes the letter was made to look like an image, such as an animal, a person, or a nature scene.

❏ On a nice piece of paper or parchment, write your name with the first letter illuminated as the monastic scribes would have done. Write the rest of your name in small, simple letters. Use gold and silver pens, paint pens, paint, gold leaf, and/or markers to decorate your letter. You can add miniature paintings and decorative borders to the page. An example of an illuminated letter can be found on p. 138 of KFH. Place your artwork in your Art, Inventions, & Architecture section.

Capetian France

GET READY For this lesson you will need:
- KFH
- Timeline

❏ Read KFH pp. 126 - 127, Capetian France.

❏ Outline these pages and title your outline "Capetian France." Place your work in the Summaries section of your binder.

❏ Record significant on your timeline:

  987 Beginning of Capetian Dynasty in France
  1328 Capetian Dynasty falls (France)

❏ Add the following to your Men & Women section along with a short summary of each:
  Hugh Capet
  Louis the Fat
  Eleanor of Aquitaine

The Crusades

GET READY For this lesson you will need:
- KFH
- TSOM (optional)
- Timeline

❏ Read KFH pp. 148 - 149, The Crusades.

❏ Outline these pages and title "The Crusades." Place your outline in the Summaries section of your binder.

❏ Read TSOM Chapter 34, The Crusades.

❏ Record the following in your Men & Women section. Include a brief description of their roles in the Crusades:
  Pope Urban II   **Louis IX of France**
  Seljurk Turks   **Walter the Penniless**
  Peter the Hermit   **Saladin**
  Richard I (Richard the Lionheart)

❏ Record significant dates on your timeline:
  1096 First Crusade
  1187 Saladin wins Jerusalem back from the Crusaders

1189	Third Crusade
1202	Fourth Crusade in Constantinople
1212	Children's Crusade
1218	Fifth Crusade
1228	Sixth Crusade
1291	Last Crusade

Lesson 33 The Crusades (cont.)

GET READY For this lesson you will need:
- KFH
- TSOM (optional)
- Map 8, The First Crusade
- Colored pencils

☐ Begin a summary of the Crusades. Start by summarizing three of the Crusades. Write a summary of the first Crusade, the third Crusade, and one more of your choice. Use information from your readings in TSOM and KFH. Place your work in the Wars & Conflicts section of your binder.

Information about the first Crusade can be found at http://academickids.com/encyclopedia/f/fi/first_crusade.html

Information about the third Crusade can be found at http://www.historyforkids.org/learn/medieval/history/highmiddle/thirdcrusade.htm

☐ Complete map 8. Label the following using KFH p. 148 and your atlas as references:

France   Rome
Holy Roman Empire Hungary
Constantinople   Jerusalem
Byzantine Empire Britain
Mediterranean Sea Palestine
the islands in the Mediterranean Sea
Draw in red the route of the Crusaders.

Lesson 34 The Crusades (cont.)

GET READY For this lesson you will need:
- KFH
- TSOM (optional)

☐ Finish your summary of the Crusades by writing a report titled "The Aftermath of the Crusades." In your report, describe the results of the crusades, including who won "The Holy Land" in the end. Also include some of the changes to Europe that occurred due to the Crusades. You can find this information in the readings found in TSOM and KFH on the crusades.

Lesson 35 Henry of Anjou

GET READY For this lesson you will need:
- Timeline
- KFH
- Colored pencils

☐ Read KFH pp. 152 - 153, Knighthood.

☐ Add the following to your Men & Women section along with a short summary of each:

Henry II
Eleanor of Aquitaine
Thomas à Becket
Richard the Lionheart (add to your former entry)
King John of England

☐ Retell the story of Henry II and Thomas Becket in your own words. Illustrate your story with a picture.

☐ Add significant dates to your timeline:

1154	Henry becomes king of England
1162	Thomas à Becket becomes Archbishop of Canterbury
1170	Murder of Thomas à Becket
1171	Henry II becomes king of Ireland
1189	Richard the Lionheart becomes King of England
1199	John becomes King of England

☐ Optional project: Create a family tree beginning with William the Conqueror and ending with Richard the Lionheart and John. When creating a family tree, use horizontal lines for marriage and vertical lines for children. For example:

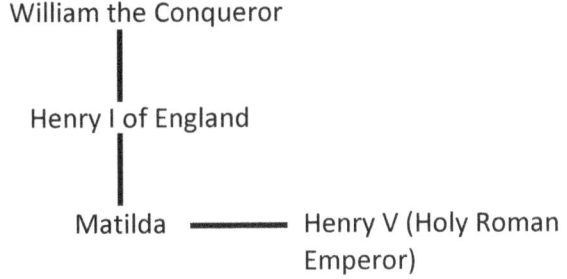

The Adventures of Robin Hood

GET READY For this lesson you will need:

- *The Adventures of Robin Hood*

☐ Read *The Adventures of Robin Hood* by Roger Lancelyn Green. Try to read 2 chapters a day.

The legend of Robin Hood is based on events surrounding the Crusades. When Richard the Lionheart was imprisoned, the English people paid taxes (they could not afford) to raise money for his release. Prince John (Richard's brother) was truly hated by most of the people of England. But most likely, Robin Hood was a fairy tale figure and not a true bandit who "robbed from the rich and gave to the poor."

After reading *Robin Hood* you may want to watch the movie titled *The Adventures of Robin Hood*. This delightful movie depicts many of the characters found in Roger Green's book and stars Errol Flynn as Robin Hood. (Warner Brothers, 1938)

Charter and Parliament

GET READY For this lesson you will need:

- KFH
- Worksheet: Medieval English Social Classes
- Colored pencils

By 1215, the nobility of England had enough of excessive taxation. When Prince John became King, he treated his subjects so poorly that he was forced into signing a charter called the Magna Carta. This document was significant because it stated that the king was not above the law. The Magna Carta upheld the feudal system and social class structure, but did limit the absolute power of the king by proclaiming individual rights of freemen. (It did little or nothing for slaves and peasants.)

☐ Read KFH pp. 162 - 163, Charter and Parliament.

☐ Outline these pages and place in the Summaries section of your binder.

☐ Add the following to your Men & Women section:

    King John of England (add to your former entry)

    Henry III

    Simon de Montfort

    Edward I

☐ Locate the worksheet titled "Medieval English Social Classes." Beginning with the King and Queen at the top of your page (the tip of the triangle) and ending with peasants at the bottom, write the English social classes in the correct order. Make your chart colorful by drawing people to represent the classes. At the base of your triangle draw many peasants (as they represented the largest class), then draw several nuns and merchants, several knights, less ladies and lords, a few bishops, and finally one king and queen at the tip of the triangle. On the right side of your chart is an upside down triangle with the widest part being next to the king and queen, and the tip on the triangle next to the many peasants at the bottom of your page. Label this triangle: "Amount of land and power." Place your work in your Summaries section.

Charter and Parliament (cont.)

GET READY For this lesson you will need:

- Timeline
- Appendix B: Magna Carta

☐ Add significant dates to your timeline:

    1215   King John signs the Magna Carta at Runnymede

1216 Henry III King of England

1265 Simon de Montford calls the 1st English Parliament

1272 Edward I King of England

1307 Edward II King of England

☐ Locate the copy of the Magna Carta in Appendix B. Try reading it, but don't worry if a lot of it is confusing. Many of the articles in the Magna Carta only pertained to the time they were written, but a few have meaning for us today. Choose five articles to summarize: choose #39 and four others. Rewrite the articles you chose in everyday language. What laws, if any, do we have that are similar to the ones you summarized. Which ones seem unfair? Which basic constitutional right we have today is similar to article #39? (If you don't know, ask an attorney!) Place your work in the Summaries section of your binder.

☐ Add the following to your Men & Women section along with a short summary of each:

St. Patrick

Brian Boru (More information about Brain Boru can be found at: www.ireland-information.com/articles/brianboru.htm)

Strongbow (Richard de Clare)

Dermot MacMurrough Kavanagh

☐ Add significant dates to your timeline:

432 St. Patrick introduces Christianity to Ireland

795 Vikings begin raiding Ireland

1014 Brian Boru defeats the Vikings in Ireland

1166 Rory O'Connor King of Ireland

1170 Strongbow and Normans invade Ireland

1530 Henry VIII imposes English control over Ireland

Lesson 39 Ireland

GET READY For this lesson you will need:

- KFH
- Map 9: Medieval Ireland
- Atlas
- Timeline

☐ Read KFH pp. 154 -155, Ireland.

☐ Outline these pages and title your outline "Ireland." Place your outline in the Summaries section of your binder.

☐ Locate map 9. Using the map on p. 154 of KFH, label water areas, label the five major kingdoms, and label The English Pale. Also label the cities of Clontarf, Dublin, and Kilkenny. Using your modern day atlas, find the cities of Cork, Limerick, and Waterford. Label these on your map. Draw two large arrows pointing at Ireland to show the invaders of Ireland. Label one arrow "Vikings A.D. 795" and one "Normans A.D. 1170."

Lesson 40 Ireland (cont.)

GET READY For this lesson you will need:

- Library access

☐ Library Trip! Choose one of the people from the last lesson to research and write a biography. Place your biography in your Men & Women section.

Lesson 41 Adam of the Road

GET READY For this lesson you will need:

- *Adam of the Road*

☐ Read *Adam of the Road* by Elizabeth Janet Gray. Try to finish this book in one week. When you have finished with the book, proceed to the next lesson for an assignment. As you read, pay attention to the main theme of this book: The importance of the individual and his ability to recognize his own talents and choose his own path in life.

Elizabeth Janet Gray wrote:

A sense of history helps us to understand the present and plan the future, and that on the worth and dignity of the individual human being, our civilization with its conception of freedom is based.

Adam of the Road (cont.)

GET READY For this lesson you will need:

- *Adam of the Road*
- Library access/ Internet
- Colored pencils

In *Adam of the Road*, Adam meets many people on his travels from several different medieval occupations including minstrel, pilgrim, squire, preacher, miller, merchant, and plowman. Some of these characters try to encourage Adam to take up their profession. But Adam makes up his own mind in the end.

- ❏ Research a medieval occupation and write a one- to two-page report. You may want to add colorful drawings to your report. You could also make and model a costume of the occupation. Take a picture of yourself and add it to your report. Place your report in your Summaries section.

www.medieval-life-and-times.info/medieval-england/medieval-jobs.htm - long list of all medieval jobs

http://prezi.com/upe2niacioud/top-five-worst-medieval-jobs/ - particularly disgusting jobs

European Trade

GET READY For this lesson you will need:
- KFH
- TSOM (optional)
- Timeline

- ❏ Trade played a very significant role in the history of the Middle Ages. Nations that did not know of each other's existence in ancient times began to communicate in the Middle Ages because of trade.

- ❏ Read KFH pp. 158 - 161, European Trade.

- ❏ Read TSOM Chapter 38, Mediaeval Trade. This reading covers the Medici and Ivan the Terrible, of whom you will study in a future lesson on the Renaissance.

- ❏ Summarize your reading by creating a list of the countries that participated in medieval trade and what they traded. Then list advances and changes that occurred to Europe because of trade (include negative and positive changes). Title your work and place it in your Summaries section.

- ❏ Add significant dates to your timeline:

    800   Begins the rise of trade in Venice
    1081   Venice trades with the Byzantine Empire
    1381   Venice dominates all trade

European Trade (cont.)

GET READY For this lesson you will need:
- KFH
- Map 10: European Medieval Trade Routes
- Atlas
- Colored pencils

❏
> On map 10, color land areas.
> Label the following:
>
> Baltic Sea   Africa   Italy   Spain
> England   France   Germany
> Mediterranean Sea   Sweden   North Sea
>
> Using KFH p. 158 as a guide, label major trading cities, and draw trade routes.
>
> Using the following information, create a map key with at least five symbols to represent the various goods traded along theses routes and others. On the map, draw the symbol on the area where the item originated (one example is drawn on the map):
>
> Asia: silk, spices, carpets, drugs, textiles
> England, Germany, and France: coal, timber, slaves, wood, iron, copper, lead
> Italy: wine, olive oil
> Africa: slaves, salt, gold, ivory, cotton
> Spain: horses, saffron
> Russia: wax, honey, rye, salmon, furs, slaves

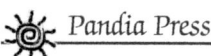

☐ Read the following primary sources about medieval trade. Read them aloud with your parent, teacher, or class. Discuss their meaning and the possible reasons why they were written.

Primary Source #1. From James I of Aragon: The Barcelona Navigation Act of 1227

Be it known to all that I, James, by the grace of God, King of Aragon, Count of Barcelona and Lord of Montpellier, am mindful of the fidelity and services which our faithful citizens of Barcelona have always shown, and do show now, to us and our predecessors. Wishing to increase your wealth by the benefits we confer on you, we have granted this special favor by our present charter to you and your successors in the city of Barcelona, namely, that any ship or vessel coming from beyond the seas, from Alexandria, or from Egypt, or proposing to go to those places from Barcelona, shall not take any merchandise or goods or cargo, nor carry them, nor bring them to those parts, while any native ship of Barcelona can, or wishes to, carry the said load or merchandise or to take it to those parts. And if any one thinks of sending his goods or merchandise to those parts let him send them in a ship or vessel of Barcelona and let him not dare to send them on a foreign ship or vessel while a ship or vessel of Barcelona is there ready to take his goods or merchandise. And we grant and concede to you, the citizens of Barcelona, that no foreign ship or other vessel, or ship from Sardinia and South Italy, shall dare to take wine at any of your quays, or buy it to take it to foreign parts, except with your permission and assent. And we have firmly ordered that the mayor, our bailiff, the honest men of Barcelona, all other mayors, bailiffs, nobles of Catalonia, officials, all our servants both now and in the future, and all those who wish to send merchandise, or to load it on ships or vessels, shall faithfully observe and cause to be observed all the privileges granted in our charter. And let no one dare to go contrary to this decree; if any do so, let them know that they will incur our anger and indignation and will pay a penalty of a thousand gold pieces. Witnesses, etc.

[From: A. de Capmany, ed., Memorias Sobre la Marina, Comercio, y Artes de la Antigua Ciudad de Barcelona, (Madrid, 1779-1792), Vol. II, p. 11; reprinted in Roy C. Cave & Herbert H. Coulson, eds.]

Primary Source #2. From William of Malmesbury: Chronicle of the Kings of England, 1065

When he [Godwin] was a young man he had Canute's sister to wife, by whom he had a son, who in his early youth, while proudly curveting on a horse which his grandfather had given him, was carried into the Thames, and perished in the stream; his mother, too, paid the penalty of her cruelty; being killed by a stroke of lightning. For it is reported, that she was in the habit of purchasing companies of slaves in England, and sending them into Denmark; more especially girls, whose beauty and age rendered them more valuable, that she might accumulate money by this horrid traffic.

Lesson 45: European Trade (cont.)

GET READY For this lesson you will need:

- *Tales from Shakespeare*
- *A Shakespeare Coloring Book*
- Colored pencils

☐ Read "The Merchant of Venice" from *Tales from Shakespeare*.

☐ Summarize this tale in your own words. Copy and color page 18 from your Shakespeare coloring book which illustrates the bargain between Shylock and Antonio. Save your summary and picture for your Shakespeare book.

Lesson 46: Medieval Architecture

GET READY For this lesson you will need:

- KFH
- Worksheet: Middle Ages Around the World
- Colored pencils

☐ Read KFH pp. 140 - 141, Architecture 501 - 1100

☐ Read KFH pp. 188 - 189, Architecture 1101 - 1460

☐ Record advances in architecture between 501 and 1460 from different parts of the world in your Art, Inventions, & Architecture section. Include several colored sketches next to your descriptions.

☐ Add information on architecture to the "Middle Ages Around the World" worksheet.

Medieval Architecture (cont.)

GET READY For this lesson you will need:
- *Castle*
- TSOM (optional)

☐ Read *Castle* by David Macaulay.

☐ Add information to your description of castles in your Art, Inventions, & Architecture section.

☐ Read TSOM Chapters 35 and 36 about Medieval cities and government.

Medieval Explorers

GET READY For this lesson you will need:
- KFH
- Map 11: Medieval Explorers
- Atlas
- Colored pencils
- Timeline

☐ Read KFH pp. 174 -175, Medieval Explorers.

☐ Write a short summary of each of the following explorers in your Men & Women section:

    Marco Polo
    Zheng He (leave room for more later)
    Ibn Battuta
    Prince Henry the Navigator (leave room for more later)

☐ Add significant dates to your timeline:

    1295   Marco Polo returns from China
    1325   Ibn Battuta begins travels
    1420   Prince Henry has Africa explored

☐ Locate map 11. Color the land areas tan. Label as many land areas (countries, cities, and towns) and water areas as you can.

With three different colors trace the routes of Marco Polo, Ibn Battuta, and Zheng He as they are presented in KFH p. 175.

Complete the Map Key for the three routes.

The Black Death

GET READY For this lesson you will need:
- KFH
- Map 12: The Black Death
- Timeline

One of the undesirable consequences of medieval trade and exploration was the spread of diseases including the Black Death which killed one third of the population of Europe and the Middle East.

☐ Read KFH pp. 178 - 179, The Black Death.

☐ On map 12, label the following, and write in dates and direction arrows indicating the spread of the Black Death.

Black Sea	England
Africa	Ireland
North Sea	Venice
Baltic Sea	Scandinavia
Paris	Southern Russia
Italy	Northern Russia
Spain	Seville
Rome	Greece
Germany	London
France	Marseille
Constantinople	Sicily
Hungary	Durham
Poland	Mediterranean Sea
Genoa	

- [ ] Add significant dates concerning the Black Death to your timeline.

The Black Death (cont.)

GET READY For this lesson you will need:
- Library access/Internet
- Drawing supplies

- [ ] Pretend you are a newspaper reporter* during the Middle Ages and you have just received the "big scoop" on the Black Death. Write a newspaper article announcing to your readers the spread and devastation of this horrible plague. Remember to write in the present tense and give your article an interesting title (it probably wasn't called the Black Death back then). You might want to speculate as to the cause of the plague and squash some of the rumors floating around. Include quotes from commoners and key rulers (you will have to research who the rulers were during the plague). You may also wish to devote an entire page to the Black Death (after all this is the big story). Include several articles on different aspects of the plague and add illustrations (pictures of rats, the town crier, or a map, for instance). Write or type your newspaper article(s) in column style like an actual newspaper. File your work in your Summaries section.

*During the Middle Ages, there weren't any newspapers. News was shouted to the public by the town crier or town herald. Many newspapers today are named "The Herald."

The Hundred Years' War

GET READY For this lesson you will need:
- KFH
- Timeline

- [ ] Read KFH pp. 176 - 177, The Hundred Years' War.

- [ ] Write a brief overall summary of The Hundred Years' War in the Wars & Conflicts section of your binder. Include dates, who was fighting, the reasons why, and the ultimate outcome. Below your summary write a brief description of the following battles (some information can be found in the picture captions):

Sluys	Agincourt
Crecy	Orléans
Poiters	

  Castillon (French recapturing their land in 1453)

- [ ] Add significant dates to your timeline.

- [ ] In your Men & Women section, write a brief description of the following people and their role in The Hundred Years' War:

Charles IV	**Philip VI**
Edward III	**John of Gaunt**
Charles VI	**Black Prince (Edward)**
Henry V	**Richard II**
Charles VII	**John, Duke of Bedford**
Joan of Arc	

The Hundred Years' War (cont.)

GET READY For this lesson you will need:
- Map 13: The Hundred Years' War
- Colored pencils
- Atlas

- [ ] On map 13, shade the areas of France that the English were trying to control (in the black outline). Complete the map key.

  In your atlas, find the city of Calais and mark this on your map. Circle this city in red and mark it as the only area the English won after a hundred years of fighting.

  Locate Paris and mark it on your map.

  Label the English Channel, the Bay of Biscay, and the North Sea.

- ☐ Next to each major battle indicated on the map, write the date the battle occurred.

  Label France, England, Spain, Atlantic Ocean, and Mediterranean Sea.

- ☐ Optional assignment: Research and write a biography on Joan of Arc. Place your work in the Religion & Mythology section of your binder.

The Canterbury Tales

GET READY For this lesson you will need:

- *The Canterbury Tales*

- ☐ Read *The Canterbury Tales* by Geoffrey Chaucer, retold by Geraldine McCaughrean. Read the introduction about Geoffrey Chaucer inside the front cover. In addition to being a poet, Geoffrey Chaucer led a busy official life, as an esquire of the royal court (serving Richard II until 1399, then Henry IV), as the comptroller of the customs for the port of London, as a participant in important diplomatic missions, and a variety of other official duties including town herald. Born in the early 1340s, he lived through the time of the Black Death and The Hundred Years' War. What you are about to read is a prose version of 13 tales from the original 24. Take a week or less to read all of the tales in this book. When you are finished, do the writing assignment in the next lesson.

Back in the Middle Ages, pilgrimages were symbolic of life. The journey to a place far away represented one's journey through life. Chaucer believed we all pilgrims on road of life and we all have stories to tell.

This world tis but a thoroughfare full of woe,
And we been pilgrims passing to and fro.
Chaucer

The Canterbury Tales (cont.)

GET READY For this lesson you will need:

- *The Canterbury Tales*
- Worksheet: Character Webs from *The Canterbury Tales*
- Worksheet: My Character Web

- ☐ Below is a character web of the Miller from *The Canterbury Tales*. Character webs help readers to better understand the characters of a story. Choose two storytellers (other than the Miller) from *The Canterbury Tales* and complete character webs for each of them on the "Character Webs from *The Canterbury Tales*" worksheet. Follow the instructions at the top of the sheet.

- ☐ When you are finished, use the "My Character Web" worksheet to create your own storyteller that could have been on the pilgrimage with Chaucer. Write the name of your storyteller in the center circle along with his or her medieval occupation. Fill in the rest of the circles with characteristics and interesting traits. Now using your character web as a guide, create a tale told by your storyteller. If you wish, you can include a prologue that gives the reader a bit of history about your character, such as Chaucer did in the prologue of *The Canterbury Tales*. Place your character webs in the Summaries section of your binder.

Part II
Asia

In Part II of this course, you will begin a non-European study of the Middle Ages and the Renaissance. The continent of Asia is a very big area; look in your atlas to see its extent. While studying history in Asia, you will be learning about vastly different cultures, including those of the Middle East, China, Japan, and Russia.

- [ ] Add important dates to your timeline:

    476   Fall of last Roman Emperor
    491   Emperor Anastasius in Constantinople
    633   Arabs conquer Syria, Egypt, & N. Africa
    976   Basil II rebuilds Byzantine Empire

Lesson 55 — The Byzantine Empire

GET READY   For this lesson you will need:
- KFH
- TSOM (optional)
- Timeline
- Map 14: The Byzantine Empire
- Colored pencils

The Byzantine Empire had influence both in Europe and Asia. Its capital, Constantinople (modern day Istanbul, Turkey), is the only city that borders two continents—Europe and Asia.

- [ ] Read TSOM Chapter 27, Rise of the Church.
- [ ] Read KFH pp. 100 - 101, The Byzantine Empire.
- [ ] Add the following men to your Men & Women section with a short summary of each:

    Constantine
    Justinian
    Anastasius
    Basil II

- [ ] On map 14, draw and shade the area controlled by the Byzantine Empire in AD 565 as indicated on p. 100 of KFH. Label the following:

Rome	Spain
Atlantic Ocean	Constantinople
Alexandria	Mediterranean Sea
Ravenna	Britain
France	Nineveh
Italy	Black Sea
Monte Cassino	Egypt
North Africa	Red Sea

Lesson 56 — Justinian

GET READY   For this lesson you will need:
- Library access

- [ ] Library Trip! Write a biography on Justinian, who played a major role in shaping the Byzantine Empire.

Lesson 57 — Islam and Baghdad

GET READY   For this lesson you will need:
- KFH
- TSOM (optional)
- Map 15: The Islamic Empire
- Colored pencils
- Atlas
- Timeline

- [ ] Read KFH pp. 106 - 107, Islam
- [ ] Read KFH p. 116, The Abbasid Dynasty
- [ ] Read TSOM Chapter 28, Mohammed.
- [ ] Create an outline on Islam. Include information from the above readings on the history of Islam and the major characteristics or beliefs. Make each major aspect of Islam a main topic in your outline. Write subtopics and details under your main topics. Title your outline and place it in your Religion & Mythology section. Your outline might begin like this:

I. Muhammad founded Islam in AD 630

   A. Muhammad was influenced by Judeo-Christian beliefs
   (add details)

B. He wrote the *Koran*.
(add details)

II. Islamic leaders are called caliphs.

  A. A caliph can order a jihad.
(add details if applicable)

  B. After Caliph Ali's murder in 661, Muslims split into two factions.
(add details)

  C. Harun al-Rashid was a powerful caliph.
(add details)

☐
> On map 15, use a modern-day atlas and other maps you have completed to label the following:
>
> | | |
> |---|---|
> | Arabian Sea | Jerusalem |
> | Constantinople | Mecca |
> | Persia | Africa |
> | Arabia | France |
> | Damascus | Black Sea |
> | Caspian Sea | Medina |
> | Baghdad | India |
> | Syria | Spain |
> | Mediterranean Sea | Red Sea |
>
> Shade the Islamic empire and the expansion of the empire, in two different colors.
>
> Draw a line from Mecca to Medina, and label it "the Hegira 622."
>
> Look in your atlas to see if the cities of Baghdad, Medina, and Mecca still exist today.
>
> Find Armenia and label it on your map.

☐ Define the *Hegira, caliph,* and *jihad* in the Religion & Mythology section of your binder.

☐ Add significant dates to your timeline:

    622   The Hegira

    630   Muhammad forms Islamic state in Mecca

    636   Muslims begin to conquer Palestine, Syria, Persia, and Egypt

    661   Muslims split into the Shiites and the Sunnis

    711   Arabs invade Spain

    750   The Abbasid dynasty begins in the Islamic Empire

    762   Baghdad founded

☐ Add The Dome of the Rock to your Art, Architecture & Inventions section along with a short summary and sketch.

Lesson 58 — Islam and Baghdad (cont.)

GET READY For this lesson you will need:

- Library access

☐ Library Trip! Research and write a biography on either Muhammad or Harun al-Rashid, and place it in your religion section.

Lesson 59 — The Seljuk Turks

GET READY For this lesson you will need:

- KFH
- Timeline
- Colored pencils
- Map 15: The Islamic Empire
- Map 14: The Byzantine Empire

☐ Read KFH pp. 134 - 135, The Seljuk Turks.

☐ In your Wars & Conflicts section, describe the battle between the Seljuks and the Byzantines at Manzikert. Remember to title your entry.

☐ Add significant dates to your timeline:

    1038   Turks conquer Afghanistan

    1055   Seljuks conquer Baghdad

| 1071 | Seljuks defeat Byzantines in Manzikert |
| 1243 | Mongols invade Seljuk empire in the Middle East |

☐ Add *Mosque* and *Minaret* to your Art, Architecture, & Inventions section along with short descriptions and sketches.

☐ On map 15 again, circle Baghdad and label "founded in 762." Label Manzikert (see KFH p. 134). Lay maps 14 and 15 side by side. Notice the region controlled by the Islamic Empire included a large section that was controlled by the Byzantine Empire in the 6th century.

One Thousand and One Arabian Nights

GET READY For this lesson you will need:

- *One Thousand and One Arabian Nights*
- Worksheet: Plot Diagram
- Appendix C: Plot Diagram

☐ Read *One Thousand and One Arabian Nights* by Geraldine McCaughrean. Try to read at least one tale a day. When you finished reading, refer back to this lesson for an assignment.

☐ On the Plot Diagram worksheet, plot one of Shahrazad's tales. In Appendix C, you will find instructions and examples of plot diagrams for two tales. Choose a different story than the ones used in the examples. Place your work in your Summaries section.

Bulgaria and Kiev

GET READY For this lesson you will need:

- KFH
- *Viking World*
- Atlas
- Timeline

Bulgaria is actually in Europe. This lesson also summarizes the rise of Kiev, a Russian city.

☐ Read KFH pp. 112 - 113, Bulgars and Slavs.

☐ Read "Sailing East" on pp. 41-42 of *Viking World* or visit www.vikinganswerlady.com/varangians.shtml

☐ In your atlas, find the countries Bulgaria, Russia, and Belarus. In Russia, locate Moscow.

☐ Write a summary paragraph on the Bulgars and the Salves. Include information on who they were, where they lived (Bulgaria or Kiev), influential leaders, Orthodox Christianity, and the influence of Byzantium and the Vikings.

☐ Add the following to your Men & Women section along with a short summary:

Rurik   **Jaroslav (Yaroslav) the Wise**

Vladimir

☐ Add two significant dates to your timeline.

Russia

GET READY For this lesson you will need:

- KFH
- Map 16: Russian Expansion 1613
- Atlas
- Colored pencils
- Timeline

☐ Read KFH pp. 226 - 227, Russia.

☐ In your Men & Women section, start a new entry titled "Russia" by making two columns. Title one column "Ivan the Great (Ivan III)" and the other "Ivan the Terrible." In the columns make a list of the characteristics and deeds of each. Do you think they deserve their names? Why do you think Ivan the Terrible has been called a man of contradiction? He was one of the most ruthless tyrants in history but is still seen as a hero by many in Russia.

☐ On map 16, shade and label the expansion of Russia up until 1613. Label the following:

Black Sea
Kiev
Caspian Sea
Moscow
Arctic Ocean
North Sea
Finland
Novgorod (look on map 5)
Norway
Sweden
Aral Sea

Compare your map with a modern day map of Russia. How has Russia grown? What country is Kiev located in today?

☐ Add significant dates to your timeline:
- 1060   Kiev declines
- 1238   Mongols invade Russia
- 1263   Expansion of Russia begins
- 1462   Ivan III strengthens Moscow
- 1472   Ivan III becomes protector of the Eastern Orthodox Church
- 1480   End of Tartar control in Russia
- 1533   Ivan the Terrible expands Russia

Lesson 63: Constantinople and the End of Byzantium

GET READY For this lesson you will need:
- KFH
- *Viking World*
- Timeline
- Map 14: The Byzantine Empire

☐ Read KFH pp. 182-183, Constantinople.

☐ Outline these pages and place your outline in your Summaries section.

☐ Read *Viking World* pp. 42 - 43 or visit www.viking.no/e/maps/ekart-osteuropa.htm about "Miklagard" (the Viking word for Constantinople)

☐ Record the following in your Men & Women section along with a short summary.

Mehmet II

Constantine XI

☐ Record significant dates on your timeline:
- 1204   Crusaders capture Constantinople
- 1453   Ottomans conquer Constantinople and change it to Istanbul

☐ On map 14 again, circle Constantinople and write "Istanbul 1453."

Lesson 64: Safavid Persia

GET READY For this lesson you will need:
- KFH
- Map 17: Safavid Persia
- Atlas
- Colored pencils

☐ Read KFH p. 209, Safavid Persia.

☐ Add the following to your Men & Women section along with a short summary:

Ismail I

Selim I

Abbas the Great

☐ On map 17, label at least 5 bodies of water plus Mesopotamia, Arabia, Tigris River, and Euphrates River. Label land areas. Draw, shade, and label the area of the Safavid Empire according to KFH p. 209. What three modern day countries now occupy the former empire of Safavid Persia? Write them in parentheses on your map.

☐ Add significant dates to your timeline:
- 1501   Beginning of the Safavid Persia Empire

1514   Safavid Persia invaded by the Ottomans

☐ Optional assignment: Do research on the Shiite Safavids and the Sunni Ottomans. Create a Venn diagram or write a summary comparing and contrasting these two Islamic groups. Include modern-day differences and similarities.

The Ottoman Empire

GET READY   For this lesson you will need:

- KFH
- Map 18: The Ottoman Empire
- Colored Pencils
- Timeline
- Library/Internet access

☐ Read KFH pp. 216 - 217, The Ottoman Empire.

☐
> On map 18, draw, shade, and label the empire at its extent in the 16th century. Label water and land areas as shown on p. 216 of KFH.

☐ Add at least three new dates to your timeline.

☐ Library trip! Summarize this lesson by writing a biography on Süleyman the Magnificent. KFH gives a great deal of information to start the biography. Include the reasons why he was called "magnificent" and information on the first Saltanas - Rose of Spring and Roxelana. Try also looking in encyclopedias and on these websites:

tp://www.nndb.com/people/916/000092640/

ww.hyperhistory.net/apwh/bios/b1suleyman.htm

ww.pbs.org/wgbh/sisterwendy/works/tug.html - ctures the tughra (signature) of Süleyman.

Sui and Tang China

GET READY   For this lesson you will need:

- KFH
- Map 19: Medieval China
- Colored Pencils
- Atlas
- Timeline

☐ Read KFH pp. 104 - 105, Sui and Tang China.

☐ Begin an outline titled "China in the Middle Ages." Create three main topics from the KFH reading. Add subtopics and details. Suggested main topics:

   I. China divided in constant warfare

   II. The Sui Dynasty

   III. The Tang Dynasty

☐ Add the following to your Men & Women section along with a short summary:

   Yang Jian (Emperor Wen)

   Yang Di

   Taizong

   An Lushan

☐
> On map 19, use KFH p. 104 as a reference and trace the Grand Canal in red. Shade, label, and date the area controlled by the Tang Dynasty c. 700. Label the Yellow River, the Yellow Sea, the South China Sea, and the Yangtze River. Write (Haung He) next to the Yellow River, (Haung Hai) next to the Yellow Sea, and (Chang Jiang) next to the Yangtze River. These are the Chinese names. In your atlas, locate this area.

☐ Record significant dates on your timeline:

   589   Yang Jian founds the Sui Dynasty in China

   618   Tang Dynasty founded in China

   907   Tang Dynasty collapses in China

☐ Add the Grand Canal to your Art, Inventions, & Architecture section along with a short summary of its history and benefits.

Lesson 67: The Song Dynasty in China

GET READY For this lesson you will need:
- KFH
- Map 19: Medieval China
- Colored Pencils
- Atlas
- Timeline

☐ Read KFH pp. 136-137, China: The Song Dynasty.

☐ Add another main topic to your outline on China (IV. The Song Dynasty). Add several subtopics and details. Leave room to add more to this outline later.

☐ Add the following to your Men & Women section:

Song Taizu   **Wang Anshi**

Kublai Khan (leave space for more later)

☐
> On map 19 again, draw, label, and date the kingdoms of China as shown on p. 136 of KFH. Label the West River (Xi Jiang).

☐ Record significant dates on your timeline:

960	Beginning of the Song Dynasty in China
1234	Mongols conquer northern China
1279	Mongols conquer southern China

Lesson 68: The Mongols

GET READY For this lesson you will need:
- KFH
- Map 20: The Mongol Empire
- Colored Pencils
- Atlas
- Timeline

For a short time, the Mongols created an empire larger than the Roman Empire. Many historians consider it the largest empire ever!

☐ Read KFH pp. 170 - 171, the Mongol Empire.

☐ Add the following to your Men & Women section along with a short summary:

Genghis Khan

Kublai Khan (add to your previous entry)

Tamerlane (Timur)

☐
> On map 20, draw, shade, and date the area of the Mongol kingdom at its height c. 1200. Using the map on p. 170 of KFH and your atlas, label at least four bodies of water and label the following countries and cities:
>
> | | |
> |---|---|
> | Russia | Japan |
> | Mongolia | Delhi |
> | Baghdad | Afghanistan |
> | Persia | The Golden Horde |
> | Syria | Tibet |
> | China | Egypt |
> | India | Greece |
> | Samarkand | Beijing (The Forbidden City) |
> | Korea | |

☐
> In your modern-day atlas, find the country of Mongolia. On map 20, draw the boundaries of modern-day Mongolia and shade this area a little darker than you shaded the Mongol Empire in the Middle Ages. Label it (Mongolia today).

☐ Add significant dates to your timeline:

1206	Genghis Khan became chief of Mongolia
1260	Mongol Empire at its greatest
1271	Kublai Khan becomes emperor of China
1275	Marco Polo visits Kublai Khan
1294	Kublai Khan dies

Lesson 69: The Mongols (cont.)

GET READY For this lesson you will need:
- Library/Internet access

☐ Write a summary of the Mongol Empire by focusing on three of its greatest leaders: Genghis Khan, Kublai Khan, and Tamerlane. Do research at your library and/or on the Internet to find out more information on the Mongol Empire. Include information that addresses the following questions:

1. How did the Mongols rise to power?
2. How were the Mongol nomads able to conquer more advanced civilizations?
3. What contributions were made by the Mongol Empire?
4. What forces led to its fall?
5. What are the Mongols like today?

Place your work in your Summaries section.

A few informative websites:

http://afe.easia.columbia.edu/mongols/

www.allempires.com/article/index.php?q=The_Mongol_Empire (detailed site)

Lesson 70: The Ming Dynasty in China

GET READY For this lesson you will need:
- KFH
- Timeline

☐ Read KFH pp. 180-181, China: The Ming Dynasty.

☐ Add to your outline on China. Add another main topic (V. The Ming Dynasty). Add subtopics and details to this main topic. Leave room to add more later.

☐ Add the following to your Men & Women section:

Hong Wu (Zhu Yuan Zhang)

Emperor Yongle

Zheng He (add to your former entry)

☐ Add the Forbidden City to your Art, Inventions, & Architecture section along with a short summary.

☐ Add significant dates to your timeline:

- 1353 Black Death comes to China
- 1368 Ming Dynasty in China
- 1517 European trade in China
- 1644 Fall of the Ming Dynasty

Lesson 71: India

GET READY For this lesson you will need:
- KFH
- Map 21: Mogul India
- Colored Pencils
- Timeline

☐ Read KFH pp. 218 - 219, India: The Moguls.

☐ Add the following to your Men & Women section along with detailed summaries:

Babur

Akbar

☐ On map 21, draw, label, and date the empires of Babur and Akbar in different colors. Complete the Map Key. Label the following:

India	Bengal
Himalayas	Delhi
Goa	Kabul
Ganges	Agra

☐ Add significant dates to your timeline:

- 1504 Moguls conquer Kabul
- 1556 Akbar begins Mogul reign

Lesson 72 — Japan

GET READY For this lesson you will need:
- KFH
- *Tales from Japan*

☐ Read KFH pp. 84 - 85, Japan.

☐ Add the following to your Men & Women section along with a short summary:

>   the Ainu
>
>   the Yayoi
>
>   the Yamato
>
>   Himiko
>
>   Prince Shotoku

☐ Add the Shinto religion to your Religion & Mythology section along with a summary.

☐ Read "The Birth of Japan" and "The Luck of the Sea and the Luck of the Mountain" in *Tales from Japan* by Helen & William McAlpine. These tales are traditional Japanese creation stories from the Shinto religion.

Lesson 73 — Fujiwara Japan

GET READY For this lesson you will need:
- KFH
- Timeline

☐ Read KFH pp. 118 - 119, Fujiwara Japan.

☐ In the Summaries section of your binder, summarize the Fujiwara period of Japan. Explain how the Fujiwara family came into power and how the family ruled through regents. (A *regent* is a person who rules in place of the actual ruler.)

☐ Add a paragraph to your Art, Inventions, & Architecture section describing the cultural advances of Fujiwara Japan. Include the *Tales of Gengi*, "The world's first novel."

☐ Add significant dates to your timeline:

>   858   Beginning of the Fujiwara period in Japan

>   1000   Peak of artistic achievement in Japan

>   1180   Gempei civil war; Minamoto shogun rise to power in Japan

☐ Add the following to your Men & Women section:

Fujiwara Yoshifusa

Lady Murasaki Shikibu

Lesson 74 — Feudalism in Japan

GET READY For this lesson you will need:
- KFH
- Map 22: Medieval Japan
- Atlas
- Colored pencils

☐ Read KFH pp. 156 - 157, Shoguns and Samurai.

☐ In the Summaries section of your binder begin a new entry titled "Japanese Feudalism." Describe the feudal society of Japan in the Middle Ages by defining the following:

>   shogun
>
>   Code of Bushido
>
>   daimyos
>
>   samurai
>
>   hara-kiri

☐ Add the following to your Men & Women section along with a short summary:

Minamoto Yoritomo

☐ Add Zen Buddhism to your Religion & Mythology section along with a short summary. When the Chinese first tried to introduce Buddhism to the Japanese, they rejected its harsh principles. So it was altered into Zen which was perceived as a gentler, kinder religion and meshed well with their ancient religion, Shinto. It became the religion of the samurai. Today many Japanese practice both Shinto and some form of Buddhism.

On map 22, use your atlas to label Japan, China, and Korea. Notice that Japan is an *archipelago* (a group of islands). Also notice how close Japan is to Korea and China, two countries that greatly influenced Japan in the past.

Using p. 84 of KFH and your atlas, label the four main islands of Japan: Hokkaido, Honshu, Shikoku, and Kyushu.

Draw an arrow from Korea to Japan and label it "ancient inhabitants & culture - 100 miles." Draw a line from China to Japan and label it "culture." Also label the following:

Pacific Ocean   Korea Strait
Edo (Tokyo)   Kyoto
Nagasaki   Sea of Japan
Mt. Fuji

The Code of Bushido:
* Loyalty to one's lord
* Denial of self
* Self sacrifice and bravery
* Live a simple life
* Control emotions
* Mental and physical discipline
* Desire an honorable death

Lesson 76: Samurai versus Knight

GET READY For this lesson you will need:
- *Tales from Japan*
- *The Story of King Arthur and His Knights*

Many comparisons have been made between medieval Japan and medieval England. Both countries are island nations protected by the sea; both had elaborate castles surrounded by towns; Yoritomo (Japan's first Shogun) was a military overlord similar to William the Conqueror; Christianity was introduced to England and Buddhism was introduced to Japan; *Tales of the Heike* were told by minstrels just like *Beowulf*. But what they had most in common was a feudal system. Just like in England, Japan had many kingdoms ruled by feudal lords who issued land to their vassals in turn for service and loyalty.

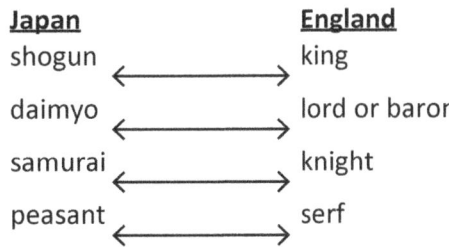

Compare a samurai to a knight by referring to past lessons and your readings from *King Arthur* and *Tales from Japan*. In your Summaries section, make a list of characteristics of a knight and a list of characteristics of a samurai. On another sheet, create a larger Venn diagram than shown on the next page. Using your lists, write the characteristics that a samurai and knight share where the two circles intersect. Write the traits that are unique outside the intersection.

Lesson 75: Tales of the Heike

GET READY For this lesson you will need:
- *Tales from Japan*

There was a turning point in Japanese history during the early part of the twelfth century. The power of the Fujiwara faded and the Gempei civil war broke out. Two warrior clans grew in power, the aristocratic Taira (the Heike) and the samurai Minamoto (the Genji). Each clan had massive armies with the Genji controlling most of eastern Japan, and the Heike having power in most of western Japan. *Tales of the Heike* is a long narrative epic that was sung and recited long before it was written down. The moral of *Tales of Heike* (the proud will surely be destroyed) comes from the Buddhist religion. The tales glorify the samurai while the proud aristocrat family is destroyed.

Read the introduction on p. 150 of *Tales from Japan*.

Read "Tales of the Heike" beginning on p. 34. As you read, look for the moral and evidence of the Code of Bushido. Bushido was based on Zen Buddhist beliefs.

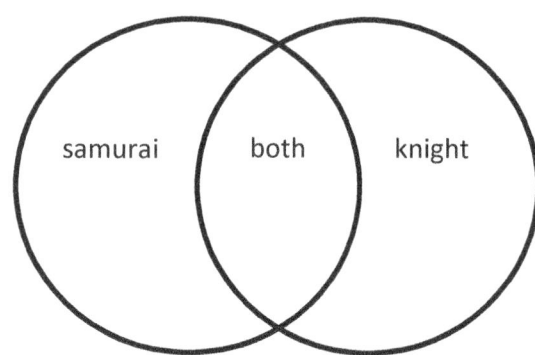

Lesson 77 — Haiku

GET READY For this lesson you will need:
- *Tales from Japan*

☐ Read the Folk and Fairy Tales section from *Tales from Japan*. When finished, return to this lesson for an assignment. As you read, see if you can detect the Shinto and Zen Buddhism beliefs that the tales are based on.

During the Renaissance, a form of poetry called *haiku* was popular in Japan. This form of poetry reflected Shinto and Zen Buddhist beliefs. A haiku does not rhyme, deals with nature and seasons, is written in the present tense, often hints of sadness, and leaves the real meaning for the reader to decipher. A haiku is a very simple poem that is only three lines long! The first line generally names the subject. The second and third lines are generally one sentence (or a sentence fragment) cut in two.

For example:

1st line is the subject:
A pine forest.

2nd & 3rd are one sentence cut in two:
Early sunset
Makes shadows.

Almost all haiku poets were samurai, and the greatest was Basho. Here is his most famous haiku:

An ancient pond.
A frog leaps;
Splash!

What does it mean? It might mean that life is not permanent, but always changing.

Another haiku by Basho:
Summer grasses -
All that remains
Of a soldier's dream.

This one might be about a samurai who once walked the earth, but now he lies beneath the grass.

☐ Write your own haiku based on one of the Japanese folktales you read. Try focusing on the Shinto and Buddhist aspects of the tale. Create a haiku about one event in the tale. Place your haiku in your Art, Inventions, & Architecture section. Here is one from "The Old Man Who Made the Trees Bloom":

Winter field.
Greedy motives
Produce old rags.

If you enjoyed writing haiku, try writing some about everyday events in your life. There are several books and websites about writing haiku.

Lesson 78 — Japan and China in the Renaissance

GET READY For this lesson you will need:
- KFH
- Timeline

☐ Read KFH pp. 232 - 233, Japan and China.

☐ Add the following to your Men & Women section along with a short summary:

Francis Xavier

Oda Nobunaga

Hideyoshi

Tokugawa Ieyasu

☐ Add the Battle of Nagashino to your Wars & Conflicts section along with a short summary. Include who was fighting, why, when, how, and the result.

History Odyssey: Middle Ages Level 2

- Add to your outline on China by adding subtopics and details to V. The Ming Dynasty.

- Add significant dates to your timeline:

    1542   Mongol invasion of China

    1549   Christian missions to Japan

    1592   Japan invades Korea (unsuccessful)

    1641   Rebel invasion of China

Lesson 79 Thailand and Vietnam

GET READY   For this lesson you will need:

- KFH
- Colored pencils
- Timeline

- Read KFH pp. 184 - 185, The Khmer Empire.

- In several paragraphs on a page in your Summaries section, summarize the Khmer Empire. Include information on devarajahs, writings, architecture, armies, occupations, food, trade, education, clothing, and their downfall.

- Below your summary, sketch a small map as shown in KFH on p. 184. Shade the area controlled by the Khmer Empire and label Vietnam, Thailand, Laos, and water areas. Find Cambodia in your atlas and label it in parentheses on your map.

- Add significant dates to your timeline:

    802   Khmer nation founded in modern-day Cambodia

    880   Khmer conquer Thailand

    1444   Khmer Empire falls after Thai invasion

Part III
The Americas

North America

GET READY For this lesson you will need:
- KFH
- Map 23: North America
- Atlas
- Timeline

☐ Read KFH pp. 110 - 111, North America 500 - 1492.

☐ Read KFH pp. 230 - 231, North America 1460 - 1600.

☐ In your Summaries section, summarize the location and characteristics of early American tribes in North America. For each area in North America listed below, record the tribes that lived there and a summary of how they lived. Use information from both readings and picture captions.

- The Southwest
- The Great Basin
- The Northwest Coast
- The Great Plains
- The Eastern Woodlands
- The Subarctic
- The Arctic

☐
> On map 23, label the geographic divisions as shown in KFH p. 231.
>
> Using your atlas, label the Mississippi River, Ohio River, Greenland, Alaska, Canada, and Mexico.
>
> Label at least three other water areas.
>
> Write the names of at least three tribes for each geographic region.

☐ Add significant dates to your timeline:

- 300 Growth of Anasazi cultures in N. America
- 800 Agricultural growth in N. America
- 1000 Anasazi Indians at their peak in N. America
- 1300 Decline of the Anasazi in N. America
- 1500 Europeans arrive on the east coast of N. America

The Maya

GET READY For this lesson you will need:
- KFH
- Map 24: Central and South America
- Worksheet: The Maya, Aztec, and Inca Empires Characteristics
- Colored pencils
- Timeline

This lesson reviews the Mayan culture which spanned from ancient times to the Middle Ages.

☐ Read KFH pp. 86 - 87, The Maya.

☐ Write characteristics of the Mayan culture on the worksheet. You will be completing this worksheet for the Aztecs and the Incas in future lessons.

☐
> On map 24, shade, label, and date the area controlled by the Maya according to the map on p. 86 in KFH. Label water areas and the following:
>
> | | |
> |---|---|
> | Chichén Itzá | Tikal |
> | Mexico | El Salvador |
> | Guatemala | the Yucatán |
> | Honduras | Peninsula |

☐ In your Art, Inventions, & Architecture section describe the Mayan city Tikal and draw a picture. Include a sketch of a pyramid-like Mayan temple.

☐ Add significant dates to your timeline:

- 300 Many cities built by Maya in Central America
- 800 Mayan civilization at its peak
- 950 Mayan culture collapses

Lesson 82: The Maya (cont.)

GET READY For this lesson you will need:
- KFH
- Map 24: Central and South America
- Timeline

☐ Read KFH pp. 128 - 129, The Americas.

☐ Add to your list of characteristics of the Maya. Include information on the invasion of the Toltec Empire and the downfall of the Maya.

☐ On map 24 again, label the following:
- Tula
- Huari
- South America

☐ Add significant dates to your timeline:

750	Teotihuacán is destroyed
800	Toltec migration into Mexico
900	Toltecs establish a city-state in Mexico
1168	Tula in Mesoamerica is destroyed
1200	Building of Mississippian temple-cities
1200	Rise of the Aztecs and Incas
1697	Last Mayan city destroyed

Lesson 83: The Aztecs and the Incas

GET READY For this lesson you will need:
- KFH
- Map 24: Central and South America
- Atlas
- Worksheet: The Maya, Aztec, and Inca Empires Characteristics
- Colored pencils
- Timeline

☐ Read KFH pp. 172 - 173, Aztecs and Incas.

☐ Add to the worksheet titled "The Maya, Aztec, and Inca Empires Characteristics" by writing characteristics on the Aztecs and the Incas.

☐ On map 24 again, label Tenochtitlan with (Mexico City) in parentheses. Find the country of Peru in your atlas and label it in parentheses on your map.

Lightly shade, label, and date the area that each empire controlled (use different colors than the Maya Empire).

☐ In your Art, Inventions, & Architecture section describe the city of Machu Picchu discovered by archeologists in 1911.

☐ Add significant dates to your timeline:

1168	Aztecs begin migration into south Mexico
1200	Inca civilization begins in S. America
1325	Aztecs build Tenochtitlan
1438	Incas begin to conquer areas of Peru
1500	Aztec Empire stretches from coast to coast in Mexico

Lesson 84: The Aztecs

GET READY For this lesson you will need:
- KFH
- Map 24: Central and South America
- Atlas
- Worksheet: The Maya, Aztec, and Inca Empires Characteristics
- Colored pencils
- Timeline

☐ Read KFH pp. 196 - 197, The Aztecs.

☐ Add characteristics to your list on the Aztecs.

☐ Add **Montezuma II** to your Men & Women section along with a short summary. Leave room to add to this entry when you study the Conquistadors.

☐ On map 24, label North America. Find Columbia on your atlas and label in parentheses on your map. Using the map on p. 196 of KFH as a reference, label, date, and increase the shaded area that the Aztecs controlled.

□ In your Art, Inventions, & Architecture section, describe the island city of Tenochtitlan. Include information from your reading in KFH from the last lesson and this lesson. Draw and color a picture of Tenochtitlan. In your picture add details such as chinampas, pyramid temples, thatched roof huts, bridges, etc.

□ Add significant dates to your timeline:

    1520   Spanish Conquistadors conquer the Aztec Empire

The Incas

GET READY For this lesson you will need:
- KFH
- Map 24: Central and South America
- Worksheet: The Maya, Aztec, and Inca Empires Characteristics
- Colored pencils
- Timeline

□ Read KFH pp. 198 - 199, The Inca Empire.

□ Add characteristics to your list on the Incas.

□ > On map 24 again, label the Andes. Using the map on p. 198 of KFH as a reference, label, date, and increase the shaded area that the Incas controlled.

□ In your Art, Inventions, & Architecture section, describe the terrace cities build by the Incas in the Andes. Add a sketch of the terraces.

□ Add the following to your Men & Women section along with a short summary:

    Sapa Inca

    Pachacuti

    Topa

    Huayna Capac

    Huascar & Atahualpa (leave room for more when you study the Conquistadors)

□ Add significant dates to your timeline:

    1450   The Inca Empire at its greatest

    1533   Spanish Conquistadors conquer the Inca Empire

The Maya, Aztecs, and Incas

GET READY For this lesson you will need:
- KFH
- Worksheet: The Maya, Aztec, and Inca Empires Venn Diagram

□ Compare and contrast the empires of the Central and South America during the Middle Ages on the worksheet titled "The Maya, Aztec, and Inca Empires Venn Diagram." Using all the information from the past several lessons (lists of characteristics, maps, images in KFH, timeline, architectural drawings, etc.), compare and contrast these three cultures on the Venn diagram. Find characteristics that were common to all three cultures, those common to two cultures, and those unique to only one culture. Write the characteristics in their appropriate place on the Venn diagram.

□ Now use your Venn diagram to write a summary comparing and contrasting these three cultures. Your summary could be two paragraphs; one describing how the cultures were alike and one describing their differences. Place the list of characteristics, the Venn diagram, and your summary in the Summaries section of your binder.

Part IV
Africa

The king adorns himself like a woman wearing necklaces around his neck and bracelets on his forearms and he puts a high cap decorated with gold and wrapped in a turban of fine cotton. He holds an audience in a domed pavilion around which stand ten horses covered with gold-embroidered materials... on his right, are the sons of the vassal kings of his country, wearing splendid garments and their hair plaited with gold. At the door of the pavilion are dogs of excellent pedigree. Round their necks they wear collars of gold and silver, studded with a number of balls of the same metal.

- Abu Abdullah al-Bakri, a 10th century geographer, referring to a king of Ghana.

Ghana, "The Land of Gold"

GET READY For this lesson you will need:

- KFH
- Map 25: African Kingdoms
- Colored pencils
- Atlas
- Timeline

❑ Read KFH p. 117, Ghana.

❑ Begin an outline on Africa with a main topic titled "Ghana." Add subtopics and details.

❑
> On map 25, outline and date the area controlled by Ghana in the Middle Ages (the area in red in KFH). Shade this area and fill in the Map Key. In your atlas, find modern-day Ghana and label it in parentheses on your map. Label the following:
>
> | | |
> |---|---|
> | Red Sea | Libya |
> | Madagascar | Mediterranean Sea |
> | Morocco | Middle East |
> | Koumbi Saleh | Sahara Desert |
> | Tangier | |
>
> Draw an arrow from Ghana toward the Middle East. Label the arrow "gold."

❑ Add significant dates to your timeline:

- 700 Ghana, Africa becomes a gold trading center
- 900 Ghana at its peak for gold and salt trade
- 1240 Ghana becomes Mali

Mali and Ethiopia

GET READY For this lesson you will need:

- KFH
- Map 25: African Kingdoms
- Colored pencils
- Atlas
- Timeline

❑ Read KFH pp. 164 - 165, Mali and Ethiopia.

❑ Continue your outline on Africa by adding two more main topics - Mali and Ethiopia. Add subtopics and details.

❑
> Referring to the map on p. 208 of KFH, outline, shade, and date the kingdom of Mali on map 25 in a different color than you shaded Ghana. Add to the Map Key.
>
> Label Timbuktu and Ethiopia.
>
> Draw an arrow from Mali towards the Middle East labeled "ivory, gold, & slaves."
>
> Look at a modern-day atlas or wall map. Do Ethiopia and Mali still exist today? How about Timbuktu? Where in Africa are they located?

❑ Add **Sundiata**, **Mansa Musa**, and the mythical **Prester John** to your Men & Women section along with short summaries.

❑ Add significant dates to your timeline:

- 1137 Founding of Ethiopia
- 1240 Sundiata founds Mali
- 1307 Mali becomes Muslim under Mansa Musa, its greatest ruler

Lesson 89: Sundiata, The Lion King

GET READY For this lesson you will need:

- Appendix D: "Sundiata, The Lion King of Mali"

☐ Read "Sundiata, The Lion King of Mali." The history of Sundiata was passed on from one generation to the next by the griot (or jali). Griots played a very important role in African history. They were the historians, storytellers, and entertainers. When you finish reading, return to this lesson for an assignment.

☐ Examine the role of the African griot. What role does the griot play in this story? What is the evidence that the story has changed over the years as it was passed on? How does the griot attempt to get himself into the story? How is the story as much entertainment as it is history? Summarize your answers to these questions in your Summaries section under the heading "The Role of Griots in African history."

Lesson 90: Benin and Zimbabwe

GET READY For this lesson you will need:

- KFH
- Map 25: African Kingdoms
- Colored pencils
- Atlas
- Timeline

☐ Read KFH pp. 166 - 167, Benin and Zinbabwe.

☐ Add to your outline on Africa with two more main topics - Benin and Zimbabwe. Add subtopics and details.

☐ On map 25 again, label Great Zimbabwe. Draw a circle around Benin and Zimbabwe. Shade and date these kingdoms and add to the map key.

Look in your atlas and see if you can locate Benin and Zimbabwe.

Label Nigeria in parentheses on the proper place on your map.

Draw an arrow form Benin to the Middle East and label it "bronze." Draw an arrow from Zimbabwe to the Middle East and label it "gold and copper."

☐ Add Great Zimbabwe to your Art, Inventions, & Architecture section along with a summary of its walled palace city.

☐ Add significant dates to your timeline:

    900   Founding of Benin, Africa

    900   Zimbabwe trading gold and copper

    140   Benin, Africa at its peak

    1500   Portuguese buying slaves from West Africa (but not Benin)

Lesson 91: Songhay

GET READY For this lesson you will need:

- KFH
- Map 25: African Kingdoms
- Colored pencils
- Atlas
- Timeline

☐ Read KFH p. 208, The Songhay Empire.

☐ Add one more main topic to your outline on Africa. Add subtopics and details.

☐ On map 25 again, outline, shade, and date the area of the Songhay Empire. Include Timbuktu and overlap the empire of Mali. Complete the Map Key.

Draw an arrow form Songhay to the Middle Eat and label it "gold and slaves."

Shade the area of the Islamic Empire.

☐ Add significant dates to your timeline:

    600   al-Yaman founds Songhay in Africa

    1200   Songhay Empire converts to Islam

1325	Songahy becomes part of Mali
1464	Songhay becomes independent & conquers Mali
1493	Songhay at its peak under Askia
1591	Moroccans conquer Songhay

Part V
Europe in the Renaissance

Lesson 92: Introduction to the Renaissance

GET READY For this lesson you will need:

- KFH
- TSOM (optional)
- Worksheet: The Renaissance Web

☐ Read KFH pp. 202 - 203, The Renaissance

☐ TSOM Chapter 39, The Renaissance.

☐ Write a summary titled "Renaissance - Rebirth." Describe who, what, when, why, how, and where the Renaissance happened. Describe who the important people of the Renaissance were, what is the Renaissance, why this was a time of rebirth and considered a transition from medieval times to modern times, how the people in the time of the Renaissance looked back and forward at the same time, and where did the Renaissance happen. Your summary should be at least a page long. This summary will be easier to write if you complete a character web on the Renaissance. Locate the worksheet titled "The Renaissance Web." This time the Renaissance is the "character." Fill in the extending circles with attributes of the Renaissance. When you write your summary, each circle could represent paragraph. Some circles could be combined into one paragraph (e.g. When and Where).

☐ Add the following people to your Men & Women section along with a short summary:

Gutenberg	**Erasmus** (save room for more later)
Savonarola	**Dante**
Petrarch	**the Medicis**
Chrysoloras	**the Borgias**

☐ Add the philosophy of humanism to your Religion & Mythology section along with a summary.

Lesson 93: Introduction to the Renaissance (cont.)

GET READY For this lesson you will need:

- *Tales from Shakespeare*
- *A Shakespeare Coloring Book*
- Colored pencils

In the last lesson, you learned that the people of the Renaissance admired the ideas and writings from ancient Greece. Shakespeare was one of those who was influenced by Homer and Virgil, and he wrote several plays that take place in Greece.

☐ Read "A Midsummer Night's Dream," "The Comedy of Errors," "Timon of Athens," and "Pericles, Prince of Troy" from *Tales from Shakespeare*.

☐ On four separate pages, retell the stories in your own words.

☐ Copy and color one or more of pages 12 - 16 in *A Shakespeare Coloring Book* depicting scenes from "A Midsummer Night's Dream." Save your summaries and coloring pages for a Shakespeare book that you will assemble later.

Lesson 94: The Spanish Inquisition

GET READY For this lesson you will need:

- KFH
- Map 26: The Reunification of Spain
- Colored pencils
- Timeline

Earlier in this course, you learned that much of Spain was under Islamic rule in the Middle Ages and that the Spanish were tolerant of other religions like Judaism. All that changed at the end of the 15th century.

☐ Read KFH pp. 200 - 201, The Reconquest of Spain.

☐ Summarize the Spanish Inquisition and the reunification of Spain in your Religion & Mythology or Summaries section.

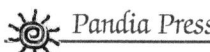

- Add the following to your men and Women section along with a short summary:

  Ferdinand   **Christopher Columbus**
  (save room for more later)

  Isabella   **Henry VIII**

  Joanna the Mad   **Catherine of Aragon**

  Charles V (save plenty of room for more in several future lessons)

- On map 26, refer to the map on p. 200 of KFH to label and draw the boundaries of the different countries that Spain was divided into before 1479.

  Shade the countries of Spain different colors.

  Label Portugal, France, Africa, the Pyrenees mountains, and the Mediterranean Sea.

  Draw a line to link Castile with Aragon and write "Unified in 1479" on the line.

  Under Granada, write "Muslim until 1492."

  Under Spain, write "Unified as one country in 1515 by Ferdinand and Isabella."

- Add significant dates to your timeline:

711	Berbers (Muslims) invade Spain from Africa
1235	Reconquest of Muslim Spain by Christians almost complete
1469	Marriage of Ferdinand and Isabella
1474	Isabella inherits Castile
1478	Spanish Inquisition begins
1479	Aragon and Castile united by Ferdinand & Isabella
1492	Christopher Columbus sails the ocean blue
1492	Reconquest of Muslim Spain by Christians complete
1504	Isabella dies
1515	Spain unites into one country
1516	Ferdinand dies

The Portuguese Empire

GET READY   For this lesson you will need:
- KFH
- Map 27: The Spanish and Portuguese Empires
- Colored pencils
- Atlas
- Timeline

- Read KFH pp. 212 - 213, The Portuguese Empire

- Outline this reading with two main topics about Portuguese seafaring and the start of the slave trade.

- Add to your entry on **Henry the Navigator** in your Men & Women section. Leave room for more on Henry in the next lesson.

- On map 27, draw and shade the empire of Portugal (as indicated in KFH). Label the following:

North America	Brazil
N. Atlantic Ocean	India
South America	China
S. Atlantic Ocean	Mozambique
Africa	Lisbon
Pacific Ocean	Goa
Asia	Calicut
Europe	Madagascar
Indian Ocean	West Indies
Spain	São Tomé
Portugal	

  Draw arrows labeled "slaves" from São Tomé to Brazil and the West Indies.

  Label Australia in parentheses because it had not been discovered at this time in history.

  On your atlas find the Canary Islands and the island of Madeira. Label these on your map.

  Label Moluccas and under it write "Spice Islands."

  Locate Indonesia in your atlas and label it on your map (also called the East Indies).

- Add significant dates to your timeline.:

    1530   1st Portuguese colony established in Brazil

    1534   1st African slaves brought to Brazil

European Explorers

GET READY   For this lesson you will need:
- KFH
- TSOM (optional)
- Encyclopedias, Internet, and/or library access

- Read KFH pp. 206 - 207, European Explorers.

- Read TSOM Chapter 41, The Great Discoveries

- Read the picture caption on p. 223 in KFH about **Sir Frances Drake**. (KFH has disappointingly little information on Sir Frances Drake. He was the first Englishman to sail around the world and played an important role in defeating the Spanish Armada. See if you can locate more information from encyclopedias or on the Internet).

- Write a summary of each of the following in your Men & Women section:

Ferdinand Magellan	**James Cartier**
John Cabot	**Henry the Navigator** (add to former entry)
Pedro de Covilham	**Vasco da Gama**
Bartholomew Díaz	**Christopher Columbus** (add to former entry)
Amerigo Vespucci	**Nicolaus Copernicus** (leave room for more later)
Sir Frances Drake	**Vasco Núñez de Balboa**

    Prester John (add to former entry)

European Explorers (cont.)

GET READY   For this lesson you will need:
- KFH
- Map 28: European Explorers
- Map 26: The Reunification of Spain
- Colored pencils
- Atlas
- Timeline

> On map 28, label the continents.
>
> Now close your books and see how many countries, cities, and bodies of water (that you have studied so far) you can label from memory. When you are finished use map 26, KFH p. 207, and your atlas to check your work and label others places along the routes of the explorers.
>
> On map 28, trace the routes of each explorer in different colors, beginning at their starting points and ending where they completed their journeys. Use KFH p. 207 for a reference. Add each explorer to the map key and include dates of their travels.

- Add significant dates to your timeline:

    1488   Bartholomew Díaz sailed around Africa

    1497   John Cabot discovers Newfoundland

    1498   Vasco da Gama reaches India

    1499   Amerigo Vespucci discovers South America

    1519   Magellan sails around Cape Horn (S. America)

    1522   Magellan's crew are the 1st to sail around the world

    1535   James Cartier sails to the St. Lawrence river for France

    1577   Sir Frances Drake sails around the world

Lesson 98 — European Explorers (cont.)

GET READY For this lesson you will need:

- Library access

☐ Library trip! Choose one of the explorers from Lessons 96 and 97 to research and write a biography. Place your report in the Men & Women section of your binder. Include a map sketch of his travels in your report.

Lesson 99 — The Conquistadors and the Spanish Empire

GET READY For this lesson you will need:

- KFH
- Map 27: The Spanish and Portuguese Empires
- Colored pencils
- Timeline

When you studied the Aztecs and the Incas, you learned about a group of Spaniards known as the Conquistadors who conquered the empires in Central and South America.

☐ Read KFH pp. 220 -221, The Conquistadores.

☐ Add the following to your Men & Women section along with a short summary:

Hernán Cortéz   **Francisco Pizarro**

Huascar & Atahualpa (add to former entry)

Philip II (save room to add more)

Montezuma II (add to former entry)

☐ Add two paragraphs to your Summaries section. Title one "The Conquistadors" and the other "The Council of the Indies." Summarize the roles of both of these groups and include their harsh treatment of the Native Americans.

☐ On map 27 again, use KFH p. 221 as a reference to draw and shade the area of the Spanish Empire (the dashed lines) a different color than you shaded the Portuguese. Label the Philippines. Complete the map key.

☐ Add significant dates to your timeline:

- 1571 Spanish conquer the Philippines
- 1600 Spanish Empire is the largest empire

Lesson 100 — The Powerful Hapsburgs

GET READY For this lesson you will need:

- KFH
- Map 29: The Hapsburgs & The Netherlands
- Colored pencils
- Timeline

☐ Read KFH p. 222, The Hapsburgs.

☐ Summarize this reading by listing all of the areas controlled by the Hapsburgs and how they obtained each one. Title your work and place it in your Summaries section.

☐ Add to your entry on **Charles V** in your Men & Women.

☐ On map 29, draw, shade, and date the areas of the Hapsburgs and the Holy Roman Empire as indicated in KFH. Complete the Map Key. Label the bodies of water and the following:

Spain	Sardinia
Portugal	Switzerland
Hungary	Naples
Africa	Sweden
Italy	France
Sicily	Germany
Austria	Norway
Denmark	Ottoman Empire

☐ Add significant dates to your timeline:

- 1506 Charles V, a Hapsburg, inherits Burgundy and the Netherlands
- 1516 Charles V inherits Spain and Naples
- 1519 Charles V becomes Holy Roman Emperor
- 1546 War between the Hapsburgs and the Protestants
- 1556 Philip II becomes king of Spain

Lesson 101: Dutch Independence

GET READY For this lesson you will need:

- KFH
- Map 29: The Hapsburgs & The Netherlands
- Atlas
- Timeline

☐ Read KFH pp. 228 - 229, Dutch Independence.

☐ Make a vertical timeline of the Netherlands. Start at the top of a page in your Summaries section and write "800 - Netherlands divided into 17 provinces ruled by various families after the collapse of Charlemagne's Empire." Under that entry write an entry for the 1300s and the 1400s, and so on until you reach 1648 at the bottom of your page.

☐ In your Men & Women section add the following along with a short summary:

Charles V (add to former entry)

Philip II (add to former entry)

William of Orange (save room to add more later)

☐ On map 29 again, draw and label the Republic of United Netherlands and Spanish Netherlands using p. 228 of KFH as a guide. Label the following:

Amsterdam   English Channel
Ireland   England
Antwerp

Do Amsterdam and Antwerp still exist today? What countries are they located in? In your atlas, locate Belgium and Luxembourg. Label these in parentheses on your map.

☐ Add significant dates to your timeline:

1516   The Netherlands become a Spanish possession
1568   Protestant revolt against the Catholic Spanish begins in the Netherlands
1576   Antwerp in the Netherlands is destroyed by the Spanish
1648   Dutch independence (the Netherlands) is recognized by Spain

Lesson 102: The Spanish Armada

GET READY For this lesson you will need:

- KFH
- Map 29: The Hapsburgs & The Netherlands
- Atlas
- Timeline

☐ Read KFH p. 223, The Spanish Armada.

☐ Summarize the Spanish Armada in your Wars & Conflicts section. Include information on who was fighting, why, where, when, and the outcome.

☐ In your Men & Women section add the following along with a short summary:

Philip II (add to former entries)

Elizabeth I (save room to add more later)

☐ On map 29 again, label Lisbon in Portugal and Calais (look in your atlas).

Draw an arrow from Lisbon to the English Channel near Calais and from England to the English Channel. Where the arrows meet, draw a little ship or an X and write "Spanish Armada - 1588."

☐ Add significant dates to your timeline:

1588   The Spanish Armada (Spain vs. England)

Visit this web site - *www.schoolhistory.co.uk/lessons/armada/map.htm* to see a neat map and reenactment of the Spanish Armada.

Lesson 103: Tudor England

GET READY For this lesson you will need:

- KFH
- Worksheet: Henry VIII's Family Tree
- Worksheet: Tudor Family Reunion

Have you heard the saying, "truth is stranger than fiction"? That was certainly the truth for the most powerful family in Renaissance England, the Tudors. The life of the Tudors had as much intrigue, romance, violence, betrayal, and surprises as a Hollywood movie.

- ☐ Read KFH pp. 210-211, Tudor England.

- ☐ Locate Henry VIII's Family Tree worksheet. On the tree branches, write in Henry VIII's wives and children. You may have to do some research to locate all of the names.

- ☐ Locate the Tudor Family Reunion worksheet. Follow the instructions found on the worksheet. Place both of your worksheets in your Men & Women section.

There are many web sites with information on the Tudors. Here are a couple you may want to check out:

www.pbs.org/wnet/sixwives - A cool web site with information on Henry's six wives.

http://englishhistory.net/tudor/contents.html - This wonderful site has primary source information from the Tudors, including letters written by the six wives, Anne Boleyn's speech at her execution, and other documents.

This is an Old English nursery rhyme concerning the fate of Henry VIII's six wives:

> *Divorced, beheaded, died*
> *Divorced, beheaded, survived*

Lesson 104 Tudor England (cont.)

GET READY For this lesson you will need:
- *Tales from Shakespeare*
- *A Shakespeare Coloring Book*
- Colored pencils

- ☐ Read "King Lear" and "Cymberline" from *Tales from Shakespeare*. Both of these tales take place in England.

- ☐ Retell each story in your own words. Copy and color pages 42 and 44 from *A Shakespeare Coloring Book*. Save your summaries and coloring pages for a Shakespeare book you will be assembling later.

Lesson 105 France

GET READY For this lesson you will need:
- KFH
- Timeline

- ☐ Read KFH pp. 224 - 225, French Wars of Religion.

- ☐ Outline this reading. Place your outline in your Summaries section or Religion & Mythology section.

- ☐ Add the following to your Men & Women section along with a short summary:

    Catherine de Médicis

    Charles IX of France

    the Guise Family

    Henry III of France

    Henry Guise

    Henry IV of France (Henry Navarre)

- ☐ Describe the Huguenot wars and War of the Three Henrys in your Wars & Conflicts section.

- ☐ Add significant dates to your timeline:

    1559 Catherine de Médicis becomes regent of France

    1562 Huguenot wars begin

    1576 Edict of Beaulieu

    1585 War of the Three Henrys begins

Lesson 106 France (cont.)

GET READY For this lesson you will need:
- *Tales from Shakespeare*
- *A Shakespeare Coloring Book*
- Colored pencils

- ☐ Read "As You Like It" and "All's Well that Ends Well" from *Tales from Shakespeare*. Both of these tales take place in France.

- ☐ Retell each story in your own words. Copy and color page 30 from *A Shakespeare Coloring Book*. Save your summaries and coloring page for a Shakespeare book you will be assembling later.

Lesson 107 The Reformation and Counter-Reformation

GET READY For this lesson you will need:
- KFH
- TSOM (optional)
- Timeline

☐ Read KFH pp. 214 - 215, The Reformation.

☐ Read TSOM Chapter 43, The Reformation and Chapter 44, Religious Warfare. (You can stop reading midway through Chapter 44, if you wish. Here Van Loon begins to discuss the Thirty Years' War which you will study next year.)

☐ Add the following people to your Men & Women section along with a short summary from both of the above readings:

Martin Luther   **John Calvin**

William of Orange (add to former entry)

Ulrich Zwingli   **Pope Paul III**

Erasmus (add to former entry)

Ignatius Loyola   **Pope Leo X**

Charles V (add to former entry)

Pope Julius II   **Ignatius of Loyola**

Philip II (add to former entry)

☐ Write a one-page summary on the Reformation. Include the events that led up to the Reformation, why it happened, where, what happened, and key players. Include information on Martin Luther's "Indulgences," Erasmus's "Praise of Folly," heretics, religious intolerance, religious tolerance, and The Diet of Worms. Place your summary in your Religion & Mythology section.

☐ Write a one-page summary on the Counter-Reformation. Include information on where, why, when, the key players, the Council of Trent, Ignatius of Loyola, and the Jesuits. Place your summary in your Religion & Mythology section.

☐ Add significant dates to your timeline.

Lesson 108 Italy

GET READY For this lesson you will need:
- KFH
- Timeline

☐ Read KFH pp. 204 - 205, Italy.

☐ Summarize the Renaissance in Italy by writing a summary on each of the three prominent families. On a page in your Summaries section titled "Renaissance Italy," make three columns. Title the first column "the Medici family," the second column "the Borgias family," and the last column "the Sforzas family." Write detailed information on each family.

☐ Add significant dates to your timeline.

Lesson 109 Italy (cont.)

GET READY For this lesson you will need:
- *Tales from Shakespeare*
- *A Shakespeare Coloring Book*
- Colored pencils

☐ Read "Romeo and Juliet," "Taming of the Shrew," "Measure for Measure," "Othello," "The Two Gentleman of Verona," "The Merchant of Venice," "Much Ado About Nothing," and "The Winter's Tales" from *Tales from Shakespeare*. These tales take place in Italy.

☐ On eight separate pages, retell the stories in your own words.

☐ In *A Shakespeare Coloring Book*, copy and color one or more of pages 10 - 11 depicting scenes from "Romeo and Juliet," page 6 depicting a scene from "Taming of the Shrew," page 40 depicting a scene from "Othello," page 7 depicting a scene from "Two Gentlemen of Verona," page 18 depicting a scene from "Merchant of Venice," page 22 depicting a scene from "Much Ado About Nothing," and page 45 depicting a scene from "The Winter's Tale." Save your summaries and coloring pages for a Shakespeare book that you will assemble later.

Lesson 110: Renaissance Art, Writings, and Inventions

GET READY For this lesson you will need:

- KFH
- TSOM (optional)
- Worksheet: The Renaissance Around the World
- Colored pencils

☐ Read KFH pp. 234 - 239, The Arts, Architecture, and Science and Technology 1461 - 1600.

☐ Read TSOM Chapter 40, The Age of Expression.

☐ Locate the worksheet titled "The Renaissance Around the World." In each box on the map, list the art, inventions, scientists, architecture, and writings that occurred during the Renaissance in that region of the world. Also include names of the inventors, artists, and writers. Use information from the readings in this lesson and other lessons. For example, don't forget to include Gutenberg, Shakespeare, and Dante. Draw a line from each box to its appropriate place on the map. Color the map and place it in your Art, Inventions, & Architecture section.

☐ Add all of the inventors, scientists, artists, and writers to your Men & Women section that you have not written about previously.

Lesson 111: Shakespeare

GET READY For this lesson you will need:

- *Tales from Shakespeare*
- *A Shakespeare Coloring Book*
- Colored pencils
- Construction paper
- Stapler

☐ Read "The Tempest," "Twelfth Night; or, What You Will," and "Hamlet, Prince of Denmark" from *Tales from Shakespeare*.

☐ On three separate sheets of paper, retell the stories in your own words.

☐ Copy and color one or more of pages 32 - 35 depicting scenes of "Hamlet," page 43 depicting a scene from "Twelfth Night," and pages 46 - 48 depicting scenes of "The Tempest" from *A Shakespeare Coloring Book*.

☐ Assemble your Shakespeare book. Gather the story summaries and coloring pages on Shakespeare that you have completed throughout this course. Assemble them in any order you wish. Create a cover for your book on construction paper, and stable the pages together along the left spine.

Lesson 112: From the Middle Ages to the Renaissance

GET READY For this lesson you will need:

- Your history binder with all your work thus far

☐ Use what you have learned about the Middle Ages and the Renaissance to choose one of these statements:

1. The Renaissance was a natural progression from the Middle Ages and was not a dramatic change.

2. The Renaissance was a dramatic change from the Middle Ages and was not a natural progression.

☐ On the top of a page in your Summaries section, write the statement that you believe most accurately describes the transition from the Middle Ages to the Renaissance. Below the statement, write several paragraphs that prove the statement. It is helpful to write down several points on a separate piece of paper; make each point a paragraph in your essay. Try to find at least three points to prove the statement. It does not matter which statement you choose; it only matters that you can support it. There is not a right or wrong choice.

Lesson 13: Timeline Analysis

GET READY For this lesson you will need:
- Worksheet: Timeline Analysis
- Timeline

You have spent the last year recording Middle Ages and Renaissance history dates from different regions of the world on your timeline. At times you have been jumping all over your timeline going back and forth from 500 to 1600. An enormous amount occurred during these 1100 years, and the easiest method to study the events was to present history one region at a time rather than chronologically skipping from one region to another. However, now that you have completed your study of the Middle Ages, it is time to analyze your timeline chronologically. You might be amazed by what you find.

☐ To do this analysis you will use the Timeline Analysis worksheets. Start at the beginning of the Middle Ages on your timeline and look at what was happening in different parts of the world for the first time span on your chart (500 - 600). Also look in the different sections of your binder for dates and on the mini timelines you created. Write these events in their proper places on your chart. Continue this for each time period. You do not need to recopy your entire timeline! That is not the purpose of this exercise. The purpose is for you to notice the similarities, connections, and great differences between events that were occurring in the world at the same time. Pick and choose those events that you feel best reflect each time span. Below is an example of what your chart might look like for the time span of 1201 to 1250. Notice the influence of the Muslims and Christians around the world in the Middle East, Africa, and Europe. Also notice that while in Europe sophisticated legislation was beginning created, in the Americas, civilization was just beginning.

☐ When you have completed the chart, choose four or five time spans where either a surprising difference, a powerful connection, or an incredible coincidence occurred. Summarize these events in paragraph form and place in the Summaries section of your binder.

Date range \ Area	Europe	The Middle East	Africa	East Asia	The Americas
1201 - 1250	Magna Carta and 4 crusades for the Holy Land	Constantinople looted by the 4th crusade	Songhay adapts Islam and Ethiopians carving rock Christian churches	Genghis Khan leader of the great Mongol Empire	Incas begin civilization

APPENDIX A

Attribution of Sources

When conducting research for the writing assignments in this course, you will be reading books and passages written by other people. If you want to use the writings of others in your summaries, essays, and your research paper, you will need to paraphrase the work or quote the author and then attribute (give credit for) the work to the author. Proper attribution of sources is very important and helps you to avoid plagiarism. Plagiarism is presenting someone else's work as your own or not properly attributing an idea to the author. Plagiarism can be a serious offense. At many colleges and high schools, students receive a failing grade if they plagiarize. Also, you should be aware that professors have sophisticated software and resources to assist them in detecting plagiarism.

PARAPHRASING AND QUOTING

Paraphrasing is restating a passage and conveying its meaning with different words. To paraphrase correctly, you need to restate the original author's ideas in your own words. Simply changing a few words in a sentence is not paraphrasing. The best way to paraphrase is to begin by thoroughly reading the passage you want to paraphrase. Then close the book and rewrite the idea without looking at the original work. Be sure to cite all of the authors and their works from which you borrowed ideas in the bibliography at the end of your report (see bibliography examples on the next page).

A quote is the exact words of the author placed in quotation marks. When using a quote, state the words exactly as the author did. Most of the time it is more appropriate to paraphrase an author than to directly quote him or her. But occasionally you will want to use a quote. You might want to use a quote when the words of the author are particularly powerful, when you are quoting a line in literature, or when using the words of a famous person. For example:

When Rousseau said, "Man is born free, and everywhere he is in chains," he implied that people are hindered by the limitations of their government.

Punctuation in quotations can be tricky. Refer to your grammar book or a writing handbook, like those published by the MLA, to learn proper punctuation when using direct quotes.

BIBLIOGRAPHY

A bibliography is a list of the books, articles, Internet sites, and audiovisuals from which you gathered information when preparing your report. When do you need to cite a source in a bibliography? Basically, you need to cite any source from which you borrow an idea, use direct quotes, or write a paraphrase in your report. You do not need to cite a source when the knowledge is common knowledge. For example, information about Napoleon that indicates he was a successful general of the French army who crowned himself emperor in 1804 does not need to be attributed because this information is common history knowledge.

When writing a bibliography, you should . . .
- Put the sources in alphabetical order by the author's last name or by the first word of the title if there is no author (not counting "a," "an," or "the").
- Indent the second line of an entry if you need to use more than one line.
- Skip a line after each entry.

ope in the Renaissance   History Odyssey: Middle Ages Level 2

Lesson 13: Timeline Analysis

GET READY For this lesson you will need:

- Worksheet: Timeline Analysis
- Timeline

ou have spent the last year recording Middle Ages and naissance history dates from different regions of the orld on your timeline. At times you have been jumping l over your timeline going back and forth from 500 1600. An enormous amount occurred during these .00 years, and the easiest method to study the events as to present history one region at a time rather than ironologically skipping from one region to another. owever, now that you have completed your study the Middle Ages, it is time to analyze your timeline ironologically. You might be amazed by what you find.

☐ To do this analysis you will use the Timeline Analysis worksheets. Start at the beginning of the Middle Ages on your timeline and look at what was happening in different parts of the world for the first time span on your chart (500 - 600). Also look in the different sections of your binder for dates and on the mini timelines you created. Write these events in their proper places on your chart. Continue this for each time period. You do not need to recopy your entire timeline! That is not the purpose of this exercise. The purpose is for you to notice the similarities, connections, and great differences between events that were occurring in the world at the same time. Pick and choose those events that you feel best reflect each time span. Below is an example of what your chart might look like for the time span of 1201 to 1250. Notice the influence of the Muslims and Christians around the world in the Middle East, Africa, and Europe. Also notice that while in Europe sophisticated legislation was beginning created, in the Americas, civilization was just beginning.

☐ When you have completed the chart, choose four or five time spans where either a surprising difference, a powerful connection, or an incredible coincidence occurred. Summarize these events in paragraph form and place in the Summaries section of your binder.

Date range \ Area	Europe	The Middle East	Africa	East Asia	The Americas
1201 - 1250	Magna Carta and 4 crusades for the Holy Land	Constantinople looted by the 4th crusade	Songhay adapts Islam and Ethiopians carving rock Christian churches	Genghis Khan leader of the great Mongol Empire	Incas begin civilization

APPENDIX A

How to Write a Biography

A biography is a story about a person's life. When you write about yourself, it is called an autobiography. A biography can be a paragraph in length or long enough to make a book. For this course, your biographies should be one to five pages in length (less if typed). Obviously, in this course, your biographies will be about people who lived a long time ago. When writing a biography on a living person, you would be wise to interview the person if possible. When writing about a person from the past, you will have to depend on primary sources, historians, and other biographers. Primary sources are especially important. A primary source is any record from the actual time period in which the person lived. A primary source could be an autobiography written by the person you are studying, documents from the time period, or writings from witnesses to the events.

The first step to writing a biography is to research the person's life. You can use encyclopedias, your local library, and/or find information on the internet. Take notes while you are researching. Locate information about the person's birth, death, childhood, good and bad deeds, obstacles he/she overcame, the effect he/she had on history, time period and environment, family and friends, and other important or interesting aspects of his/her life.

Next, decide how you want to write the biography and make an outline from your notes. A biography can be written in linear fashion by starting at the person's birth and continuing with events in chronological order, ending with his/her death. You may choose to write about one important aspect or event in the person's life or focus on a few different themes. The choice is yours. Organize your notes by completing an outline. Write each major point in a biography as a main topic. Each main topic should be a paragraph in your biography. Then organize the details under each main topic.

The last step to writing a biography is to create a true story. Biographies are much more interesting when told as a story with characters, plot, conflict, and emotion that brings the person to life. Use your outline to guide your writing. Finally, give your biography a title and show off your work!

For more information on writing an interesting biography see The Biography Maker at
http://www.fno.org/bio/biomaker.htm

APPENDIX A

Attribution of Sources

When conducting research for the writing assignments in this course, you will be reading books and passages written by other people. If you want to use the writings of others in your summaries, essays, and your research paper, you will need to paraphrase the work or quote the author and then attribute (give credit for) the work to the author. Proper attribution of sources is very important and helps you to avoid plagiarism. Plagiarism is presenting someone else's work as your own or not properly attributing an idea to the author. Plagiarism can be a serious offense. At many colleges and high schools, students receive a failing grade if they plagiarize. Also, you should be aware that professors have sophisticated software and resources to assist them in detecting plagiarism.

PARAPHRASING AND QUOTING

Paraphrasing is restating a passage and conveying its meaning with different words. To paraphrase correctly, you need to restate the original author's ideas in your own words. Simply changing a few words in a sentence is not paraphrasing. The best way to paraphrase is to begin by thoroughly reading the passage you want to paraphrase. Then close the book and rewrite the idea without looking at the original work. Be sure to cite all of the authors and their works from which you borrowed ideas in the bibliography at the end of your report (see bibliography examples on the next page).

A quote is the exact words of the author placed in quotation marks. When using a quote, state the words exactly as the author did. Most of the time it is more appropriate to paraphrase an author than to directly quote him or her. But occasionally you will want to use a quote. You might want to use a quote when the words of the author are particularly powerful, when you are quoting a line in literature, or when using the words of a famous person. For example:

When Rousseau said, "Man is born free, and everywhere he is in chains," he implied that people are hindered by the limitations of their government.

Punctuation in quotations can be tricky. Refer to your grammar book or a writing handbook, like those published by the MLA, to learn proper punctuation when using direct quotes.

BIBLIOGRAPHY

A bibliography is a list of the books, articles, Internet sites, and audiovisuals from which you gathered information when preparing your report. When do you need to cite a source in a bibliography? Basically, you need to cite any source from which you borrow an idea, use direct quotes, or write a paraphrase in your report. You do not need to cite a source when the knowledge is common knowledge. For example, information about Napoleon that indicates he was a successful general of the French army who crowned himself emperor in 1804 does not need to be attributed because this information is common history knowledge.

When writing a bibliography, you should . . .
- Put the sources in alphabetical order by the author's last name or by the first word of the title if there is no author (not counting "a," "an," or "the").
- Indent the second line of an entry if you need to use more than one line.
- Skip a line after each entry.

APPENDIX A

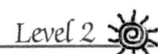

- Underline the title of a book or magazine (or use italics if typing).
- List the authors in the order they are listed on the title page when there is more than one author.
- List the title of an article from a newspaper of encyclopedia before the name of the newspaper or encyclopedia. Put titles of articles in quotation marks.

BIBLIOGRAPHY EXAMPLES*

BOOK:
Author's last name, first name. *Title of book*. Place of publication: Publisher, copyright year.

Example:
Yates, Elizabeth. *Amos Fortune, Free man*. New York: Puffin Books, 1950.

ENCYCLOPEDIA ARTICLE WITHOUT AN AUTHOR:
"Title of article." *Name of encyclopedia*. Edition number. Copyright year.

Example:
"Civil War Heroes." *World Book Encyclopedia*. 10th ed. 1999.

MAGAZINE OR NEWSPAPER ARTICLE:
Article author's last name, first name. "Title or headline of article." *Name of magazine or newspaper*. Date of magazine or newspaper, section and page.

Example:
Jacobs, Ernie. "War Casualties Rise." *New York Times*. May 10th, 2007, A1.

INTERNET ADDRESS:
Author's last name, first name. "Title of item." Date of document or download. http://address
If there is no author cited, then begin with the title.

Example:
"BookRags Short Guide on Kidnapped." January 29, 2007. www.bookrags.com/shortguide-kidnapped

FILM:
Title of film. Director. Distributor, year of release.

Example:
It's a Wonderful Life. Dir. Frank Capra. RKO, 1946.

* According to the MLA. Gibaldi, Joseph. *MLA Handbook for Writers of Research Papers*. 6th ed.

APPENDIX B

Magna Carta

Runnymede, June 15th, 1215

John, by the Grace of God, King of England, Lord of Ireland, Duke of Normandy and Aquitaine, and Earl of Anjou, to his Archbishops, Bishops, Abbots, Earls, Barons, Justiciaries, Foresters, Sheriffs, Governors, Officers, and to all Bailiffs, and his faithful subjects,

-Greeting.

Know ye, that We, in the presence of God, and for the salvation of our own soul, and of the souls of all our ancestors, and of our heirs, to the honor of God, and the exaltation of the Holy Church and amendment of our Kingdom, by the counsel of our venerable fathers, Stephen Archbishop of Canterbury, Primate of all England, and Cardinal of the Holy Roman Church, Henry Archbishop of Dublin, William of London, Peter of inchester, Joceline of Bath and Glastonbury, Hugh of Lincoln, Walter of Worcester, William of Coventry, and Benedict of Rochester, Bishops; Master Pandulph our Lord the Pope's Subdeacon and familiar, Brother Almeric, Master of the Knights-Templars in England, and of these noble persons, William Mareschal Earl of Pembroke, William Earl of Salisbury, William Earl of Warren, William Earl of Arundel, Alan de Galloway Constable of Scotland, Warin Fitz-Gerald, Hubert de Burgh Seneschal of Poictou, Peter Fitz-Herbert, Hugh de Nevil, Matthew Fitz-Herbert, Thomas Basset, Alan Basset, Philip de Albiniac, Robert de Roppel, John Mareschal, John Fitz-Hugh, and others our liegemen; have in the First place granted to God, and by this our present Charter, have confirmed, for us and our heirs for ever:

(1) That the English Church shall be free, and shall have her whole rights and her liberties inviolable; and we will this to be observed in such a manner, that it may appear from thence, that the freedom of elections, which was reputed most requisite to the English Church, which we granted, and by our Charter confirmed, and obtained the Confirmation of the same, from our Lord Pope Innocent the Third, before the rupture between us and our Barons, was of our own free will: which Charter we shall observe, and we will it to be observed with good faith, by our heirs for ever. We have also granted to all the Freemen of our Kingdom, for us and our heirs for ever, all the underwritten Liberties, to be enjoyed and held by them and by their heirs, from us and from our heirs.

(2) If any of our Earls or Barons, or others who hold of us in chief by military service, shall die, and at his death his heir shall be of full age, and shall owe a relief, he shall have his inheritance by the ancient relief; that is to say, the heir or heirs of an Earl, a whole Earl's Barony for one hundred pounds: the heir or heirs of a Baron for a whole Barony, by one hundred pounds; the heir or heirs of a Knight, for a whole Knight's Fee, by one hundred shillings at most: and he who owes less, shall give less, according to the ancient custom of fees.

(3) But if the heir of any such be under age, and in wardship, when he comes to age he shall have his inheritance without relief and without fine.

(4) The warden of the land of such heir who shall be under age, shall not take from the lands of the heir any but reasonable issues, and reasonable customs, and reasonable services, and the without destruction and waste of the men or goods, and if we commit the custody of any such lands to a Sheriff, or any other person who is bound to us for the issues of them and he shall make destruction or waste upon the ward- lands we will recover damages from him and the lands shall be committed to two lawful and discreet men of that fee, who shall answer for the issues to us, or to him to whom we have assigned them. And if we shall give or sell to any one the custody of any such lands, and he shall make destruction or waste upon them, he shall lose the custody; and it shall be committed to two lawful and discreet men of that fee, who shall answer to us in like manner as it is said before.

(5) But the warden, as long as he hath the custody of the lands, shall keep up and maintain the houses, parks, warrens, ponds, mills, and other things belonging to them, our of their issues; and shall restore to the heir when he comes of full age, his whole estate, provided with ploughs and other implements of husbandry, according as the time of Wainage shall require, and the issues of the lands can reasonably afford.

(6) Heirs shall be married without disparagement, so that before the marriage be contracted, it shall be notified to the relations of the heir by consanguinity.

(7) A widow, after the death of her husband, shall immediately, and without difficulty have her marriage and her inheritance; nor shall she give any thing for her dower, or for her marriage, or for her inheritance, which her husband and she held at the day of his death: and she may remain in her husband's house forty days after his death, within which time her dower shall be assigned.

(8) No widow shall be compelled to marry herself, while she is willing to live without a husband; but yet she shall give security that she will not marry herself without our consent, if she hold of us, or without the consent of the lord of whom she does hold, if she hold of another.

(9) Neither we nor our Bailiffs, will seize any land or rent for any debt, while the chattels of the debtor are sufficient for the payment of the debt; nor shall the sureties of the debtor be compelled, while the principal debtor is able to pay the debt; and if the principal debtor fail in payment of the debt, not having wherewith to discharge it, the sureties shall answer for the debt; and if they be willing, they shall have the lands and rents of the debtor, until satisfaction be made to them for the debt which they had before paid for him, unless the principal debtor can shew himself acquitted thereof against the said sureties.

(10) If any one hath borrowed any thing from the Jews, more or less, and die before that debt be paid, the debt shall pay no interest so long as the heir shall be under age, of whomsoever he may hold; and if that debt shall fall into our hands, we will not take any thing except the chattel contained in the bond,

APPENDIX B

(11) And if any one shall die indebted to the Jews, his wife shall have her dower and shall pay nothing of that debt; and if children of the deceased shall remain who are under age, necessaries shall be provided for them, according to the tenement which belonged to the deceased: and out of the residue the debt shall be paid, saving the rights of the lords (of whom the lands are held.) In like manner let it be with debts owing to others than Jews.

(12) No scutage nor aid shall be imposed in our kingdom, unless by the common council of our kingdom; excepting to redeem our person, to make our eldest son a knight, and once to marry our eldest daughter, and not for these, unless a reasonable aid shall be demanded.

(13) In like manner let it be concerning the aids of the City of London.- And the City of London should have all it's ancient liberties, and it's free customs, as well by land as by water.- Furthermore, we will and grant that all other Cities, and Burghs, and Towns, and Ports, should have all their liberties and free customs.

(14) And also to have the common council of the kingdom, to assess and aid, otherwise than in the three cases aforesaid: and for the assessing of scutages, we will cause to be summoned the Archbishops, Bishops, Abbots, Earls, and great Barons, individually, by our letters.- And besides, we will cause to be summoned in general by our Sheriffs and Bailiffs, all those who hold of us in chief, at a certain day, that is to say at the distance of forty days, (before their meeting,) at the least, and to a certain place; and in all the letters of summons, we will express the cause of the summons: and the summons being thus made, the business shall proceed on the day appointed, according to the counsel of those who shall be present, although all who had been summoned have not come.

(15) We will not give leave to any one, for the future, to take an aid of his own free-men, except for redeeming his own body, and for making his eldest son a knight, and for marrying once his eldest daughter; and not that unless it be a reasonable aid.

(16) None shall be compelled to do more service for a Knight's-Fee, nor for any other free tenement, than what is due from thence.

(17) Common Pleas shall not follow our court, but shall be held in any certain place.

(18) Trials upon the Writs of Novel Disseisin, Of Mort d'Ancestre (death of the ancestor), and Darrien Presentment (last presentation), shall not be taken but in their proper counties, and in this manner:- We, or our Chief Justiciary, if we are out of the kingdom, will send two Justiciaries into each county, four times in the year, who, with four knights of each county, chosen by the county, shall hold the aforesaid assizes, within the county on the day, and at the place appointed.

(19) And if the aforesaid assizes cannot be taken on the day of the county-court, let as many knights and freeholders, of those who were present at the county-court remain behind, as shall be sufficient to do justice, according to the great or less importance of the business.

(20) A free-man shall not be fined for a small offence, but only according to the degree of the offence; and for a great delinquency, according to the magnitude of the delinquency, saving his contenement: a Merchant shall be fined in the same manner, saving his merchandise, and a villain shall be fined after the same manner, saving to him his Wainage, if he shall fall into our mercy; and none of the aforesaid fines shall be assessed, but by the oath of honest men of the vicinage.

(21) Earls and Barons shall not be fined but by their Peers, and that only according to the degree of their delinquency.

(22) No Clerk shall be fined for his lay-tenement, but according to the manner of the others as aforesaid, and not according to the quantity of his ecclesiastical benefice.

(23) Neither a town nor any person shall be compelled to build bridges or embankments, excepting those which anciently, and of right, are bound to do it.

(24) No Sheriff, Constable, Coroners, nor other of our Bailiffs, shall hold pleas of our crown.

(25) All Counties, and Hundreds, Trethings, and Wapontakes, shall be at the ancient rent, without any increase, excepting in our Demesne-manors.

(26) If any one holding of us a lay-fee dies, and the Sheriff or our Bailiff, shall shew our letters- patent of summons concerning the debt which the defunct owed to us, it shall be lawful for the Sheriff or our Bailiff to attach and register the chattels of the defunct found on that lay-fee, to the amount of that debt, by the view of lawful men, so that nothing shall be removed from thence until our debt be paid to us; and the rest shall be left to the executors to fulfil the will of the defunct; and if nothing be owing to us by him, all the chattels shall fall to the defunct, saving to his wife and children their reasonable shares.

(27) If any free-man shall die intestate, his chattels shall be distributed by the hands of his nearest relations and friends, by the view of the Church, saving to every one the debts which the defunct owed.

(28) No Constable nor other Bailiff of ours shall take the corn or other goods of any one, without instantly paying money for them, unless he can obtain respite from the free will of the seller.

(29) No Constable (Governor of a Castle) shall compel any Knight to give money for castle-guard, if he be willing to perform it in his own person, or by another able man, if he cannot perform it himself, for a reasonable cause: and if we have carried or sent him into the army, he shall be excused from castle-guard, according to the time that he shall be in the army by our command.

(30) No Sheriff nor Bailiff of ours, nor any other person shall take the horses or carts of any free-man, for the purpose of carriage, without the consent of the said free-man.

(31) Neither we, nor our Bailiffs, will take another man's wood, for our castles or other uses, unless by the consent of him to whom the wood belongs.

(32) We will not retain the lands of those who have been convicted of felony, excepting for one year and one day, and then they shall be given up to the lord of the fee.

(33) All kydells (wears) for the future shall be quite removed our of the Thames, and the Medway, and through all England, excepting upon the sea-coast.

(34) The writ which is called Praecipe, for the future shall not be granted to any one of any tenement, by which a freeman may lose his court.

(35) There shall be one measure of wine throughout all our kingdom, and one measure of ale, and one measure of corn, namely the quarter of London; and one breadth of dyed cloth, and of russets, and of halberjects, namely, two ells within the lists. Also it shall be the same with weights as with measures.

(36) Nothing shall be given or taken for the future for the Writ of Inquisition of life or limb; but it shall be given without charge, and not denied.

(37) If any hold of us by Fee-Farm or Socage, or Burgage, and hold land of another by Military Service, we will not have the custody of the heir, nor of his lands, which are of the fee of another, on account of that Fee-Farm, or Socage, or Burgage; nor will we have the custody of the Fee-Farm, Socage or Burgage, unless the Fee-Farm owe Military Service. We will not have the custody of the heir, nor of the lands of any one, which he holds of another by Military Service, on account of any Petty-Sergeantry which he holds of us by the service of giving us daggers, or arrows, or the like.

(38) No Bailiff, for the future, shall put any man to his law, upon his own simple affirmation, without credible witnesses produced for the purpose.

(39) No freeman shall be seized, or imprisoned, or dispossessed, or outlawed, or in any way destroyed; nor will we condemn him, nor will we commit him to prison, excepting by the legal judgement of his peers, or by the laws of the land.

(40) To none will we sell, to none will we deny, to none will we delay right or justice.

(41) All Merchants shall have safety and security in coming into England, and going out of England, and in staying and in travelling through England, as well by lands as by water, to buy and sell, without any unjust exactions, according to ancient and right customs, excepting the time of war, and if they be of a country at war against us: and if such are found in our land at the beginning of a war, they shall be apprehended without injury of their bodies and goods, until it be known to us, or to our Chief Justiciary, how the Merchants of our country are treated who are found in the country at war against us; and if ours be in safety there, the others shall be in safety in our land.

(42) It shall be lawful to any person, for the future, to go out of our kingdom, and to return, safely and securely, by land or by water, saving his allegiance to us, unless it be in time of war, for some short space, for the common good of the kingdom: excepting prisoners and outlaws, according to the laws of the land, and of the people of the nation at war against us, and Merchants who shall be treated as it is said above.

(43) If any hold of any escheat, as of the Honor of Wallingford, Nottingham, Boulogne, Lancaster, or of other escheats which are in our hand, and are Baronies, and shall die, his heir shall not give any other relief, nor do any other service to us, than he should have done to the Baron, if that Barony had been in the hands of the Baron; and we will hold it in the same manner that the Baron held it. 44) Men who dwell without the Forest, shall not come, for the future, before our Justiciaries of the Forest on a common summons; unless they be parties in a plea, or sureties for some person or persons who are attached for the Forest.

(45) We will not make Justiciaries, Constables, Sheriffs, or Bailiffs, excepting of such as know the laws of the land, and are well disposed to observe them.

(46) All Barons who have founded Abbies, which they hold by charters from the Kings of England, or by ancient tenure, shall have the custody of them when they become vacant, as they ought to have.

(47) All Forests which have been made in our time, shall be immediately disafforested; and it shall be so done with Water-banks, which have been taken or fenced in by us during our reign.

(48) All evil customs of Forests and Warrens, and of Foresters and Warreners, Sheriffs and their officers, Water-banks and their keepers, shall immediately be inquired into by twelve Knights of the same county, upon oath, who shall be elected by good men of the same county; and within forty days after the inquisition is made, they shall be altogether destroyed by them never to be restored; provided that this be notified to us before it be done, or to our Justiciary, if we be not in England.

(49) We will immediately restore all hostages and charters, which have been delivered to us by the English, in security of the peace and of their faithful service.

(50) We will remove from their bailiwicks the relations of Gerard de Athyes, so that, for the future they shall have no bailiwick in England; Engelard de Cygony, Andrew, Peter, and Gyone de Chancell, Gyone de Cygony, Geoffrey de Martin, and his brothers, Philip Mark, and his brothers, and Geoffrey his nephew, and all their followers.

(51) And immediately after the conclusion of the peace, we will remove out of the kingdom all foreign knights, cross-bow-men, and stipendiary soldiers, who have come with horses and arms to the molestation of the kingdom.

APPENDIX B

(52) If any have been disseised or dispossessed by us, without a legal verdict of their peers, of their lands, castles, liberties, or rights, we will immediately restore these things to them; and if any dispute shall arise on this head, then it shall be determined by the verdict of the twenty-five Barons, of whom mention is made below, for the security of the peace.- Concerning all those things of which any one hath been disseised or dispossessed, without the legal verdict of his peers by King Henry our father, or King Richard our brother, which we have in our hand, or others hold with our warrants, we shall have respite, until the common term of the Crusaders, excepting those concerning which a plea had been moved, or an inquisition taken, by our precept, before our taking the Cross; but as soon as we shall return from our expedition, or if, by chance, we should not go upon our expedition, we will immediately do complete justice therein.

(53) The same respite will we have, and the same justice shall be done, concerning the disafforestation of the forests, or the forests which remain to be disafforested, which Henry our father, or Richard our brother, have afforested; and the same concerning the wardship of lands which are in another's fee, but the wardship of which we have hitherto had, occasioned by any of our fees held by Military Service; and for Abbies founded in any other fee than our own, in which the Lord of the fee hath claimed a right; and when we shall have returned, or if we shall stay from our expedition, we shall immediately do complete justice in all these pleas.

(54) No man shall be apprehended or imprisoned on the appeal of a woman, for the death of any other man than her husband.

(55) All fines that have been made by us unjustly, or contrary to the laws of the land; and all fines that have been imposed unjustly, or contrary to the laws of the land, shall be wholly remitted, or ordered by the verdict of the twenty-five Barons, of whom mention is made below, for the security of the peace, or by the verdict of the greater part of them, together with the aforesaid Stephen, Archbishop of Canterbury, if he can be present, and others whom he may think fit to bring with him: and if he cannot be present, the business shall proceed, notwithstanding, without him; but so, that if any one or more of the aforesaid twenty-five Barons have a similar plea, let them be removed from that particular trial, and others elected and sworn by the residue of the same twenty-five, be substituted in their room, only for that trial.

(56) If we have disseised or dispossessed any Welshmen of their lands, or liberties, or other things, without a legal verdict of their peers, in England or in Wales, they shall be immediately restored to them; and if any dispute shall arise upon this head then let it be determined in the Marches by the verdict of their peers: for a tenement of England, according to the law of England; for a tenement of Wales, according to the law of Wales; for tenement of the Marches, according to the law of the Marches. The Welsh shall do the same to us and to our subjects.

(57) Also concerning those things of which any Welshman hath been disseised or dispossessed without the legal verdict of his peers, by King Henry our father, or King Richard our brother, which we have in our hand, or others hold with our warrant, we shall have respite, until the common term of the Crusaders, excepting for those concerning which a plea had been moved, or an inquisition made, by our precept, before our taking the cross. But as soon as we shall return from our expedition, or if, by chance, we should not go upon our expedition, we shall immediately do complete justice therein, according to the laws of Wales, and the parts aforesaid.

(58) We will immediately deliver up the son of Llewelin, and all the hostages of Wales, and release them from their engagements which were made with us, for the security of the peace.

(59) We shall do to Alexander King of Scotland, concerning the restoration of his sisters and hostages, and his liberties and rights, according to the form in which we act to our other Barons of England, unless it ought to be otherwise by the charters which we have from his father William, the late King of Scotland; and this shall be by the verdict of his peers in our court.

(60) Also all these customs and liberties aforesaid, which we have granted to be held in our kingdom, for so much of it as belongs to us, all our subjects, as well clergy as laity, shall observe towards their tenants as far as concerns them.

(61) But since we have granted all these things aforesaid, for GOD, and for the amendment of our kingdom, and for the better extinguishing the discord which has arisen between us and our Barons, we being desirous that these things should possess entire and unshaken stability for ever, give and grant to them the security underwritten; namely, that the Barons may elect twenty-five Barons of the kingdom, whom they please, who shall with their whole power, observe, keep, and cause to be observed, the peace and liberties which we have granted to them, and have confirmed by this our present charter, in this manner: that is to say, if we, or our Justiciary, or our bailiffs, or any of our officers, shall have injured any one in any thing, or shall have violated any article of the peace or security, and the injury shall have been shown to four of the aforesaid twenty-five Barons, the said four Barons shall come to us, or to our Justiciary if we be out of the kingdom, and making known to us the excess committed, petition that we cause that excess to be redressed without delay. And if we shall not have redressed the excess, or, if we have been out of the kingdom, our Justiciary shall not have redressed it within the term of forty days, computing from the time when it shall have been made known to us, or to our Justiciary if we have been out of the kingdom, the aforesaid four Barons, shall lay that cause before the residue of the twenty-five Barons; and they, the twenty-five Barons, with the community of the whole land, shall distress and harass us by all the ways in which they are able; that is to say, by the taking of our castles, lands, and possessions, and by any other means in their power, until the excess shall have been redressed, according to their verdict; saving harmless our person, and the persons of our Queen and children; and when it hath been redressed, they shall behave to us as they have done before.

And whoever of our land pleaseth, may swear, that he will obey the commands of the aforesaid twenty-five Barons, in accomplishing all the things aforesaid, and that with them he will harass us to the utmost of his power: and we publicly and freely give leave to every one to swear who is willing to swear; and we will never forbid any to swear. But all those of our land, who, of themselves, and of their own accord, are unwilling to swear to the twenty-five Barons, to distress and harass us together with them, we will compel them by our command, to swear as aforesaid.

And if any one of the twenty-five Barons shall die, or remove out of the land, or in any other way shall be prevented from executing the things above said, they who remain of the twenty-five Barons shall elect another in his place, according to their own pleasure, who shall be sworn in the same manner as the rest.

In all those things which are appointed to be done by these twenty-five Barons, if it happen that all the twenty-five have been present, and have differed in their opinions about any thing, or if some of them who had been summoned, would not, or could not be present, that which the greater part of those who were present shall have provided and decreed, shall be held as firm and as valid, as if all the twenty-five had agreed in it: and the aforesaid twenty-five shall swear, that they will faithfully observe, and, with all their power, cause to be observed, all the things mentioned above.

And we will obtain nothing from any one, by ourselves, nor by another, by which any of these concessions and liberties may be revoked or diminished. And if any such thing shall have been obtained, let it be void and null: and we will never use it, neither by ourselves nor by another.

(62) And we have fully remitted and pardoned to all men, all the ill-will, rancor, and resentments, which have arisen between us and our subjects, both clergy and laity, from the commencement of the discord. Moreover, we have fully remitted to all the clergy and laity, and as far as belongs to us, have fully pardoned all transgressions committed by occasion of the said discord, from Easter, in the sixteenth year of our reign [i.e., 1215], until the conclusion of the peace.

And, moreover, we have caused to be made to them testimonial letters-patent of the Lord Stephen, Archbishop of Canterbury, the Lord Henry, Archbishop of Dublin, and of the aforesaid Bishops, and of Master Pandulph concerning this security, and the aforesaid concessions.

(63) Wherefore, our will is and we firmly command that the Church of England be free, and that the men in our kingdom have and hold the aforesaid liberties, rights, and concessions, well and in peace, freely and quietly, fully and entirely, to them and their heirs, of us and our heirs, in all things and places, for ever as is aforesaid.

It is also sworn, both on our part, and on that of the Barons, that all the aforesaid shall be observed in good faith, and without any evil intention. Witnessed by the above, and many others.

APPENDIX C

Plot Diagram

A **Plot Diagram** is an organizational tool to help a reader recognize important parts that keep a story moving and make it interesting. It was originally developed by Aristotle in 350 BC! Most stories can be plotted on a plot diagram. Your job is to identify the parts known as the exposition, the rising action, the climax, the falling action, and the resolution. Definitions of each of these terms are provided below.

Protagonist = The main character or main group of characters in a story. Often the protagonist is the hero, but not always.

Antagonist = The character (characters) who poses problems for the protagonist. Often, the antagonist is the villain, but not always.

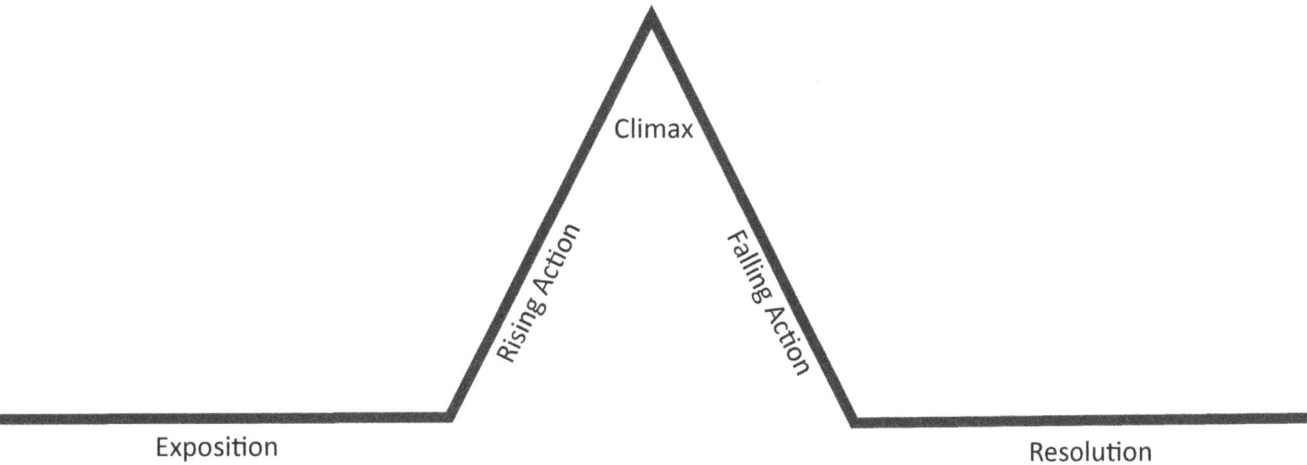

| The **Exposition** provides the background information about the protagonist, antagonist, and the setting. The exposition often ends with a single incident that indicates trouble has begun. | In the **Rising Action**, the first conflicts become complicated by other conflicts that frustrate the protagonist. | The **Climax** of the story is the turning point. It marks a change for the better. (In tragedies things get worse at the climax.) | The **Falling Action** occurs as the conflicts start to unravel and the protagonist starts winning (or losing, in a tragedy). | The **Resolution** is the story's end. The protagonist lives "happily ever after." In the case of a tragedy, the protagonist is worse off than he/she was at the exposition. |

APPENDIX C

Plot Diagram Examples from *One Thousand and One Arabian Nights*

Example #1: "The Fisherman and the Bottle"

Protagonist = fisherman
Antagonist = jinni

- Climax: The fisherman outwits the jinni, and the jinni gets back into the bottle
- Rising action: The jinni threatens to kill the fisherman
- Falling action: The fisherman throws the jinni back into the sea.
- Exposition: An old and poor fisherman prays to Allah for his catch. One day he catches a jinni in a bottle.
- Resolution: The fisherman escapes death and warns others.

Example #2: "The Everlasting Shoes" - a tragedy

Protagonist = Abu Kassim
Antagonist = big, smelly, old shoes

- Climax: Abu's shoes cost him all of his money.
- Rising action: Abu's shoes cause him to be beaten, arrested, and other misfortunes.
- Falling action: Abu becomes hysterical and disowns his shoes
- Exposition: Abu Kassim is a miser who has big, smelly, old shoes.
- Resolution: Abu curses all shoes everywhere; he leaves barefoot, and becomes a laughing stock.

APPENDIX D

"Sundiata, The Lion King of Mali"

This story is told by a jali - or griot - an oral historian of Mali, West Africa. Sundiata (also known as Sundyata) was an actual person, the first King of Mali, born about 1210 A.D. The Battle of Karina (told about at the end of the story) took place in 1235 A.D. This version is abridged and adapted from three written versions of the Epic of Sundiata and with information from Yacine Kouyate from Mali. [Text copyright, 2001 by Nick Bartel]

Part One: The Jali Speaks

I am a jali, master of the art of eloquence, descendant of the royal historians. Since time immemorial my family has been in the service to the princes of Mali. We are the vessels of history and hold in our minds the secrets of many centuries. Through our speech we bring to life the valiant deeds of kings to younger generations. I teach kings the history of their ancestors so the lives of the ancients may guide them. I shall teach you your history so you may be guided, too. I shall teach you of our time of greatness. The past is only the seed of the future.

Listen, children of Mali. Don't doubt my words. What I say is what was told to me by my father, as was told by his father to him, and so on through the generations. We are sworn to pass on our stories as we learned them.

Now listen to the story of Sundiata, the Lion King of Mali, as it was told from time beyond memory. Sundiata, the father of the bright country, the master of a hundred conquered kings! Sundiata, great among kings, and peerless among men, beloved of Allah for he was the last of the great conquerors! Sundiata, the greatest in a great line of kings.

The first kings of Mali were not indigenous. They came from the East and were descendants of a faithful servant of the Prophet Muhammad, may the peace of Allah be upon him. It was this lineage that held the power and they were initiated into the arts of hunting and healing. It was through them that their people conquered the neighboring lands and they became kings of a vast empire known as Mali.

From this noble line came Maghan, the handsome, father of Sundiata. Maghan had three wives and six children - three boys and three girls. His first wife was the beautiful Sassouma. The second wife was Sogolon, the Buffalo Woman, the mother of Sundiata.

Return now to the time before Sundiata the great Lion King was born, before he united the territories and ethnic groups of Mali into a mighty empire. Return to the savanna along the river before Sundiata's mother and father had met.

Part Two: The Prediction

King Maghan was renowned for his good looks in every land, but he also was a good king and loved by all the people. In his capital of Niani he loved to sit under the great shading arms of the silk-cotton tree which dominated the royal yard of his great clay palace. Here he could enjoy the shade and the breeze during the hottest times. Unlike his subjects, he could not go down to the river to get cool. As was the custom, the king would only present himself to the people on special occasions, so he was somewhat isolated within the royal fences.

His jali was with him singing his praises while playing on a three-stringed guitar. Servants waited upon him and fanned him, chasing away the flies. Maghan's beautiful wife Sassouma was in the palace, pregnant with their second child. His only son Dankaran was already eight years old and often came to sit on the ox-hide beside his father.

As he sat in the shade of the mighty silk-cotton tree, a hunter from far away approached carrying an offering of meat. (Since the hunter had killed an animal on the king's land, he was obligated by custom to give the king part of the animal.) His garments were covered with cowry shells which showed him to be a master in the art of hunting. He wore a reddish-brown skull cap over his gray hair braided in the fashion of the hunters of that land. These hunters were known as great soothsayers, or fortune tellers, as well. The man walked up to the king and bowed. "I salute you, King, and bring you part of the animal I have killed on your land."

The jali of the king spoke for his master. "Welcome stranger, and thank you for observing our customs. You have traveled far, sit and share with us some stories of our neighboring lands."

The hunter came and sat down upon a mat. He said, "I am not a teller of tales. I do not spin adventurous yarns, nor trick my listeners with a golden tongue. But I can boast of being a seer among the best."

He took twelve cowry shells out of his hunter's bag, raised them to his mouth and murmured an incantation. Then he threw the shells before him on the mat. He looked at them for a long time studying the way they fell and the patterns they made. Then he addressed the king. "Oh, great ruler, our world is full of mystery. Great things come from small. This silk-cotton tree springs from a tiny seed. Kingdoms are like trees; some will become like this great silk-cotton tree, and others will remain like dwarf palms. Mighty rivers begin as small streams. And who can recognize in the little child the great king to come? Know this, King Maghan. Your land is about to emerge from the night."

The jali of the king was puzzled and said, "Hunter, your words are strange. Make them as clear to us as the savannas of our land."

"Oh, King. Listen to my message. Your successor is not yet born," he said trying to avoid the eyes of the king who looked apprehensively at his son while stroking his beard. "I see two hunters coming to your city. They have come from afar. A woman comes with them. Oh, that woman! She is ugly. On her back is a hump giving her the appearance of a buffalo. Her eyes are misshapen, too. But this is the woman you must marry, for she will be the mother of the one who will make the name of your family immortal. This son will be mightier than all who have preceded him."

The hunter picked up his cowry shells and returned them to his bag. "I am only passing through, and now I must return."

The king laughed as if to appear that he was not listening deeply to the hunter's words and he said, "Don't you have any other stories for a king?"

The hunter replied, "I have spoken not to entertain, sire. But only after you sacrifice a red bull calf and let his blood sink deep into the soil, will this girl come. Farewell, great king. I am but a passing stranger."

The hunter disappeared down the trail, but the king did not forget his words and later that day ordered the sacrifice of the red bull calf. Gossip of the stranger's words were spread throughout the palace.

News of this prediction were met with fear by Sassouma, the queen and mother of eight-year-old Dankaran, whom she wanted to become the next king. The seer's words were as disturbing to her as they were attractive to her husband. Did Maghan not want to be remembered as the father of powerful rulers? Did he not want to take more wives and have more children? Such were the thoughts of the king and queen.

Part Three : Maghan and Sogolon

King Maghan was once again seated under the silk-cotton tree. It was a hot day, and his beautiful wife Sassouma had brought some water to him and sat down to enjoy the shade. She had given birth to a daughter almost two years before, and she had regained her beauty. Her attention was now on her husband and their happiness together.

Two young hunters and a young maid approached. The queen got up and went inside the palace as was required of her when strangers came. A flash of anxiety swept through her when she saw the woman covered by a veil coming down the path between the two hunters. Would her husband remember the prediction made long ago?

When the strangers were a few steps from the king, they bowed. "Great king, we are hunters from far away. The young girl is from Daw and we present her to you, for we think she is worthy to be a king's wife."

The girl was kneeling in front of the king with a veil hiding her face. Bowing, she could not conceal the hump which deformed her shoulders and back.

The king and his jali knew this extraordinary woman was the one prophesied. She must become the king's wife and mother of his son! So the king ordered a gift of kola nuts for the young hunters for bringing her to the king. The hunters were also given two beautiful maidens of the king's village to take home as their own wives.

The date of the wedding was set for next Wednesday, a lucky day, and throughout the twelve villages of the kingdom the drums announced the marriage. All the important dignitaries were invited. The royal family gave out gifts to celebrate the wedding: rice, clothes, and even gold. Oxen were sacrificed. Each village sent a troupe of dancers and musicians to participate in the celebration of the second marriage of the king.

Sogolon, the Buffalo Woman, stayed with an old aunt of the king until the wedding. In preparation she received the finest care and pampering. Along the river's edge she sang and bathed with her age-mates, who would become like sisters to her. She got marriage advice from old married women while they gave her a ritual hot-then-cold bath: "In marriage there are beautiful days, and inevitably there will be bad days. Your dignity as a woman makes it imperative that you accept either kind with a smile. If you drink honey water with your husband, be prepared to drink the bitter herbs as well. This will make certain the success of your children in this life and your place in heaven in the next."

Her hair was braided and her skin was oiled and perfumed. Throughout the night before the wedding there was a great feast by the women. It was intended to give the departing maiden a final happy memory that she would be able to fall back upon in moments of anguish during her future life as a wife and mother. Sogolon was weeping alone in the center of a circle of her friends as the rooster crowed that morning. Today she would no longer be a girl and her life as a woman would begin.

She was dressed completely in white with a large veil over her head. Her age-mates sang the bride's departure song punctuated with clapping.

Her wedding day had come. Perched on a horse she headed a procession down the path towards the palace. Women flanked her path and viewed everything and sang; it has always been so. Men had no say in the matter, and were pushed to the back.

As was the custom, during the procession cousins of the groom picked the bride up and ran off carrying her on their shoulders to the palace as the crowd cheered. The bride had been delivered to her husband. Outside the palace walls the celebrations continued, and the dancers and singers were rewarded. More gifts were distributed. The celebration continued throughout the day and night.

Part Four: Sundiata - Birth & Early Childhood

Sassouma, King Maghan's first wife, resented her husband for taking another wife even though the Qur'an allowed it. "How could you?" she cried to her husband. "Do you prefer that ugly buffalo to me?"

Maghan said, "Woman! Woman! Don't worry, I love you still. I am only trying to make an alliance with the people of

APPENDIX D

Daw. To make up for it, go and take ten cows from my herd. They are yours! But I beg you, don't disrupt my marriage to her."

Sassouma angrily departed, but plotted against Sogolon with a few of her closest friends who knew witchcraft. When she heard that Sogolon was pregnant, her jealousy became blind, and she planned to poison the Buffalo Woman and her child. But on the way to the house of Sogolon, she saw three owls descend to the roof to protect the expectant mother. She knew that nothing could be done with the owls as sentinels, so she bided her time. "Very well then," she said. "Let the child be born and we'll see... Her child will be much more vulnerable than she."

Near the moment of delivery the sky grew dark with clouds even though it was the dry season. The sun was hidden and two cyclones appeared in the sky as if in battle, twisting and confronting each other. Thunder and lightning crackled and everyone ran for shelter. Rain started falling and blanketed the earth. And then the rain stopped suddenly and the sun appeared. It was at the very moment the midwife came out of Sogolon's house to announce to Maghan that he was the father of a boy.

Drums announced the birth of a boy throughout the village and in celebration singers and balafons carried the praises of the king and his new son. The king rejoiced in his new son: child of the lion and child of the buffalo and panther! He opened six granaries and distributed rice throughout the village. Later he went to see his new son and wife along with his jali. They were amazed to see that the child had a full set of teeth and eyes that focused upon whoever was in the room! "Truly this is a good omen," the jali said. Both mother and father were so proud.

On the eighth day after the child's birth the naming ceremony was held. The jali spoke before the crowd in praise of this child and gave a prayer to Allah: "May Allah grant him long life! ["Amen!"] May Allah grant him good health! ["Amen!"] May Allah make him a good king! ["Amen!"] Then the female jalis shouted the child's multiple names selected carefully to carry his proud lineage from his great-great-grandfather through his father and mother. But the name which he was called and remembered by was "Sundiata" - the lion king. His many names were whispered in his ear so that he may remember them. The king sacrificed sheep and bulls and distributed their meat along with rice bread to the cheering villagers. The feast was the largest in memory.

But Allah has mysteries which no one can understand. Some will be lucky and live an easy life untouched by sorrow. Others will be marked for suffering. You can do nothing about it. Such is the will of Allah.

The infant Sundiata had a slow and difficult childhood. At the age of three he still crawled, dragging himself along the ground like a crocodile crawling on a sandbank. He had none of the beauty of his father: a head so big that he seemed unable to support it, large eyes which stared widely whenever anyone entered his mother's house. He did little other than sit in the middle of the house, except when he was hungry and he would drag himself out to rummage about in search of food among the calabashes waiting to be washed. He seemed to be always in a bad mood and scared other children away. He spoke little and his serious little face never relaxed into a smile.

Malicious tongues began to wag. What three-year-old has not yet taken his first steps? Why could he not speak? What three-year-old was not the center of attention receiving and returning the love of those around him? Was this the great son prophesied, or was that a cruel joke on the king? Or was there witchcraft involved?

The king's first wife rejoiced in Sundiata's infirmity. Her own son, Dankaran, was already eleven. He was a fine boy and had even begun his initiation and manhood training. Whenever she passed by Sogolon she would make comments like, "I prefer a son who walks on his two legs to a lion that crawls on the ground!" And she would laugh a wicked laugh that went straight through Sogolon.

Sogolon was greatly troubled by her son's infirmity. She tried all her talents as a sorceress, but to no avail. Nothing she did could strengthen her son's legs: no herbs, no ointments, no magical incantations.

The king himself lost hope in Sundiata. How impatient man is! Perhaps if he had another son? he thought. It was during this time that Sogolon became pregnant again, but brought forth only a daughter.

The years passed and still Sundiata did not walk, nor did he seem to try! The king wondered, "Could Sundiata possibly be the one for whom the hunter had predicted such a glorious future?"

King Maghan and his jali again went to the blacksmith soothsayer. This time he used two flat stones to help him see beyond the mysteries of this world. Feeling the stones he said, "When the seed germinates growth is not always easy. Great trees grow slowly, but they plunge their roots deep into the ground. Your son has three guardian spirits in one body: the lion, buffalo, and panther. He is not yet able to assimilate them. Be patient."

But the king continued to feel deceived and ridiculed on account of Sundiata. He took a third wife at this time, even though he was now old. This wife produced a son. But even this did not make him happy. And sadly, too, this wife died leaving her infant, named Manding Bory, motherless. Sassouma would have nothing to do with him, but Sogolon took him as her own and raised the child as Sundiata's brother.

Maghan died never seeing his son Sundiata walk. And with the death of Maghan, the eldest, the son of Sassouma, was named as king, as was the custom. And Sassouma became powerful in her new position, as well.

Sassouma no longer considered the seven-year-old Sundiata a threat, but her hatred for Sogolon continued unrelenting. Sogolon, her daughter and Sundiata, and Manding Bory were driven into the poorest section of the palace. They received only meager portions of food, the leftovers from Sassouma's meals.

APPENDIX D

One day Sogolon tried to be kind to Sassouma and went to her home asking for some baobab leaves to season a stew of chicken feet. Sassouma smugly said, "My son, for whom no great destiny was prophesied, but who can walk, run, and jump, brings me baobab leaves every day! Whereas yours, supposed to be superhuman, drags himself around like a lizard and can't even gather leaves for you! Here, take these. Go and feed your good-for-nothing son! Make him big and fat!" She laughed that diabolical laughter which jealous women know how to use so well, and threw the leaves at Sogolon.

Sogolon felt wretched and turned saying to herself, "I would rather my children and I starve to death than take the baobab leaves if we must accept her insults with them!" She covered her face to hide her tears and hurried back to her house.

Sundiata, playing on the floor of their house, saw his mother come in. "What's the matter, mother?" he asked sensing her troubled spirit. She said nothing, but her muffled cries told him everything. He felt great pity for her. Resolutely he announced, "Today I am going to walk."

Rejoice! Today would be like no other day! Today was a day of destiny. The blacksmith soothsayer knew... a huge iron rod was brought by six blacksmith apprentices and dropped outside Sundiata's hut.

Sundiata crawled on all fours to the iron rod. Sogolon followed him out of her hut. A small crowd started gathering near the iron rod. He picked it up with little difficulty and stood it vertically. Then he pulled himself up on his knees.

"Arise, young lion! Roar! And let the bush know that from now on it has a master!" cried the blacksmith.

Among the crowd was Sassouma who stood with her arms crossed and with a haughty smile. Sundiata's sister, and even Sassouma's daughter Nana, encouraged him to stand until she was silenced by her mother! Then a deadly silence gripped all those present.

Sundiata lowered his head as if examining his feet. Then he riveted his stare at the rod. The next moment his muscles swelled, and embracing the rod, he hauled himself up, his head thrown back, his eyes half closed, his teeth clenched. His legs pulled under him and they started trembling, like rice stalks whipped by the wind. In a supreme effort he managed to stretch himself completely upright; then, releasing the rod he found himself planted on his own two legs!

Soon the silence turned to joy. There was chanting and clapping! And with every step the crowd praised him more! *

Not far from the palace was a baobab tree. It was toward that tree that Sundiata slowly stumbled, leading a cheering crowd. Once there he turned to his mother and said, "Mother! Did you ask your son for some leaves?" Then with a mighty tug he uprooted the tree, put it over his shoulder, and carried it back in front of his mother's hut where he dropped it. "From this day on, it is from in front of your hut that the women of our town, including Sassouma, shall come to get their supply of leaves!"

The lion had awakened.

* Chanting of Sogolon to Sassouma: "Water in a hole, do not compare yourself with the water of the spring. The water of the spring is fresh and clear. The water in the hole is stagnant and stinks!"

Part Five: The Subas (Powerful Sorceresses)

Sundiata was now ten and a boy full of strength. His arms had the strength of ten and he inspired fear in grown men. He already had that authoritative way of speaking which belongs to those destined to rule.

From his mother he was taught the secrets of the animals and medicinal plants, and of magic. The son of his father's jali, Balla Faseke, became his own jali who taught Sundiata the history of his people and the rules of warrior's conduct. Sundiata grew in popularity from day to day, and he was surrounded by a gang of children the same age as himself.

And every day Sassouma's hatred of Sogolon and Sundiata increased. She became more and more apprehensive about her own son's throne. Even now at the age of eighteen, her son Dankaran was weak and under the influence of his mother. Sassouma really ruled in his name. And she wanted to kill Sundiata.

One night Sassouma met with the nine great suba sorceresses of Mali. When the nine old hags were seated in a semicircle around her, she said, "You who rule supreme at night and have nocturnal powers, oh you who can put an end to one's life, will you help me? I want to kill Sundiata. His destiny runs counter to my son's."

"Mother of the king," replied one suba. "Sundiata has done us no wrong. Why should we bring about his death?"

"You are wrong. He and his mother are evil and have no respect for you. Tomorrow go to his mother's vegetable patch where Sundiata stands guard. You will see how vicious he is."

"That's a clever idea," said one of the suba sorceresses. They agreed to test Sundiata and the queen gave them a reward of grain from the royal granaries and cows from the royal herds.

Sundiata got up the next morning and met with his companions. They decided to go out hunting for the day. On his way home he passed his mother's vegetable patch. There he found the nine old women stealing vegetables. They pretended to run away like thieves who had been caught red-handed.

"Stop, stop, you poor old women. Don't run. This garden belongs to all," he said. Then he and his companions filled the gourds of the old hags with vegetables. "Each time you need food," he told them, "come back and take what you need without fear."

The old women stood in amazement. "We came here to test you, Sundiata. We have no need of your vegetables. We can do nothing against a heart full of kindness. Forgive us." "Beware of the queen mother. She wishes you harm." Then the nine subas disappeared into the night.

When Sundiata returned home, he told his mother what had happened. Sogolon knew that her son's life was threatened. She would have to be more careful and use more of her magical powers to protect him. That night two guardian owls returned and perched at their doorway to prevent the harmful magic of others.

When Sassouma learned that Sundiata was still alive and protected by guardian owls, she knew that the magic of Sogolon and Sundiata was too powerful. She had to find another way to get rid of him.

Part Six: Departure from Niani

Within a year it became time for Sundiata to go into manhood training. For months, Sundiata and boys of his age were initiated into the secret knowledge of the master hunters and warriors. With him was Balla Faseke, his jali, who further trained him in the knowledge of leadership and nobility. They became closest friends and they knew that their destinies were intertwined.

One day when Sundiata was out on a hunting trip, Sassouma once again saw an opportunity to be rid of her son's rival. She told Dankaran, "We will send Balla Faseke, Sundiata's jali and friend, away from him. We can send him to the king of Sosso on a mission. Sundiata cannot question that! And he will be left without his true friend and advisor. Out of anger and humiliation he will leave our village."

"Mother," Dankaran asked, "are you sure? Balla Faseke is known for his wisdom. Is it right to take him away from my brother and send him to Sosso? The king of Sosso is a very cruel man, and Balla Faseke may not survive!"

"You are king now, and don't even know a threat to your rule! When Sundiata grows up, do you think he will not compete with you? Get rid of him now while you still can."

When Sundiata returned and heard about Dankaran's decision, he confronted his half-brother the king. He remained calm, but his eyes flashed angrily. Any other twelve-year-old child would have lost his courage in front of armed guards with drawn swords! But he grabbed his brother by the collar and said, "You have stolen my jali given to me by our father King Maghan. If you needed to send someone to Sosso, why didn't you send your own jali?"

Dankaran was angered and intimidated by his question. "I am the king now!" Sassouma had spoken to him so often that he was ashamed to tremble before a youngster. He thought of stamping him out like a black beetle. "You must leave here," he finally shouted, and Sundiata left the palace.

Sogolon heard the news. "Yes, let us leave here," she said. "Sundiata, you will return to reign when you are a man, for that is your destiny." Then she prepared her daughter and her adopted son, Manding Bory, to leave the next morning.

At the second crowing of the rooster, they left their hut with their possessions on their backs. Sundiata surrounded himself with a wall of silence as they departed. But Sogolon turned toward Sassouma's room in the palace and shouted, "Ever since the death of my husband, my children and I have been the victims of your bullying. You ridiculed my son when he couldn't walk, tried to use magic against him, and now you have taken away his jali. What else do you have in mind? We will never know, because now we will leave. The palace and the whole city of Niani are yours alone!"

In her resentment, Sogolon's voice carried throughout the palace and beyond, but Sassouma stayed silent and fearful within.

Sogolon turned her eyes to the heavens and said, "Ever since I was married thirteen winters ago, there has been no end to our suffering and humiliation!"

They left Niani without saying farewell to anyone. Their hearts were too sad for leave-takings.

They tasted the bitterness of exile. Their feet plowed up the dust of the path as they walked. They suffered insults from their countrymen. Doors were shut against them and they were chased away from each village. No one dared to help them for fear of the queen. As they trudged down the path they were escorted only by a chorus of crickets.

Part Seven: Exile - Finding Enemies and Building Allies

Two days' journey downstream on the River Niger, they came to the home of the sorcerer king of Djeliba. They were greeted pleasantly enough in words, but the welcome was full of mistrust. Yet, it is the custom to offer hospitality to travelers, so the king invited them to stay.

The palace had 70 spacious rooms arranged in a maze and thick walls. Oil lamps lit the labyrinth of this mysterious, dark palace. There were many servants, and Sogolon's family was made comfortable.

It was here they settled. Sundiata and his brother Manding Bory became friends with the other children of the palace. They enjoyed games and hunting with the other boys. But even with the kindness and hospitality they received in Djeliba, they felt torn between their present and past homes.

Three months later secretly two messengers came to the palace. They were from Queen Sassouma with a promise of gold if the king killed Sundiata. All this was overheard by a daughter of the king, and a friend of Sundiata and Manding Bory.

Early the next day she went to find Manding Bory. "Late last night," she said, "messengers spoke to my father about Sundiata. They came from Mali and offered my father much gold. I didn't hear all they said."

"I can imagine," Manding Bory replied. He knew he had to warn his brother of a plot on his life.

"Tonight my father will surely call Sundiata to a game of wori," she continued. "He is a great sorcerer and his power is in the game of wori. His skills were revealed to him by guardian spirits. Don't tell my father anything I have said, or he will kill me!" Then she ran back to the palace.

From a distance Sundiata was watching his younger brother with the princess and teased him. "I see you are fond of the daughter of the king!"

Manding Bory responded with a laugh, "If you want to tame the lion, you must be on good terms with the lion cub!"

The two boys continued exchanging proverbs, for men's knowledge is contained there. When children use proverbs well, it is a sign they have learned wisely from their elders.

Sure enough, that night Sundiata was called to the king's inner chamber. On the walls were outstanding weapons and magical fetishes. In the middle of the room was the king seated on a cow hide. In front of him was a game board with small pebbles. Unafraid Sundiata entered the dimly lit room. He was moving toward his destiny and did not know what fear was.

"What beautiful weapons you have, sire," he said. He seized a sword and began to fence with it against an imaginary foe. The king was astonished and watched the skills of the extraordinary child. Then the young prince put the sword back and said, "You sent for me, and I am here."

"Sit down," said the king. "It is my habit to invite my guest to play at wori. But I have an unusual condition. If I win -- and I will surely win -- I kill you."

Without being upset, Sundiata responded confidently, "And if I win?"

"In that case," the king laughed, "I will give you what you wish. But you should know that I always win."

"All I ask for is that sword hanging on your wall," Sundiata replied.

"Very well," said the king and began to put four pebbles into each of the holes. As he did this, he chanted:

"Wori is the invention of a hunter,
I am unbeatable in this game.
I am called the exterminator king."

And Sundiata, taking the pebbles from another hole, continued the chant as he took his turn:

"In the past guests were honored.
Gold came only yesterday.
But I came before."

"Someone has betrayed me!" the king roared knowing that Sundiata had learned of his deadly plot.

"No, king. Do not accuse anyone," said the child. "It is nearly three moons that I have been living with you and you never suggested a game of wori before. Allah protects the guest."

Confused and shaken by being discovered in a sinister plot, the king said, "You have won, but you will not have what you asked for! And I turn you out of my town. Leave at once."

Sundiata rose and bowed politely while staring calmly at the nervous king. "Thank you for your hospitality for almost three months. But I will return," he said glancing again at the sword. Then he turned and left.

So once again Sogolon and her children trod the path of exile. Suffering under the heat of day and the chill of night, they finally arrived at Tabon. This region is in the mountains and is inhabited by blacksmith magicians and warriors. The king of Tabon was old and wise. He had heard of the family's difficulties. He advised them to seek the protection of a caravan of Arab merchants who were leaving in a few days for Ghana. In the meantime, they were welcomed into the palace as honored guests.

Sundiata struck up a special friendship with Fran Kamara, the son of the king and heir to the throne. Fran Kamara invited the boys on a hunting party. Out in the bush, the youngsters talked like men.

"When I go back to Mali," Sundiata said, " I will pass through Tabon and we will go victoriously to Mali together. Between that time and now, we will have grown up."

"The army of Tabon will be under my command by then," Fran Kamara said. "And blacksmiths are excellent warriors."

"I will make you a great general," Sundiata said. "We will travel through many kingdoms and emerge the strongest of all."

The exiled family took to the road again. The king of Tabon had given them horses and the caravan headed north across the savanna to where the sands cover the land.

Tabon was very far from Ghana, but the merchants were very good to Sogolon and her family. It was during this long trip that Sundiata heard about the powerful king of Sosso, Sumangaru, whom he would fight one day. Sundiata knew that his jali, Fasso Berete, had been sent to Sosso. He learned that Sumangaru was the richest and most powerful king, and even the king of Ghana had to pay him tribute. He was also a man of great cruelty.

Once in the kingdom of Ghana, they came to the city of Wagadou. The king greeted them by saying, "Welcome royal family of Mali. My palace is your palace. The friendship which unites Ghana and Mali goes back to a very distant age. We are cousins."

In the comforts of the palace Sogolon recovered quickly from her exhaustion. But after a year she became ill. The king decided to send Sogolon to his cousin, the king of Mema. Mema was the capital of a great kingdom on the River Niger not far from Daw, Sogolon's first homeland. Surely, he thought, the air from the river would restore her health.

APPENDIX D

Traveling with merchants by camel caravan, the family got accustomed to riding the animals which were unknown in Mali. Always eager to learn, Sundiata asked the caravan travelers many questions. They were well-informed people. Sundiata learned about the lands beyond Ghana, the lands of the Arabs, and of his own ancestor, Bilal, the faithful servant of the Prophet Muhammad. He learned also about Alexander the Great, conqueror of a vast empire. But it was with terror that the merchants spoke of Sumangaru of Sosso who robbed merchants of everything when he was in a bad mood.

Before arriving at Mema, a great escort was sent out to meet the travelers. Archers and spearmen formed in a double line to welcome Sogolon and her family. They were given rooms in a wing of the great palace.

As usual, Sundiata made his presence felt among the young princes of Mema, and he gained their respect and friendship. The king himself could hardly take his eyes off the young prince. He had no son of his own, and was impressed by the greatness and confidence of someone so young. Could this be his adopted heir?

Years passed and Sundiata grew. His body became stronger and he shot up like a young tree. His misfortunes had made his mind wise.

The King of Mema recognized in Sundiata great strength and leadership. He asked Sundiata to join him as a warrior. Sundiata was as agile as a panther, as noble as a lion, and as ready to attack as a buffalo. By eighteen years of age, Sundiata had already proven himself a great warrior. The King of Mema, who had no son of his own, thought of Sundiata as his own successor.

But as Sundiata grew stronger, his mother Sogolon became weaker. One day Sogolon called Sundiata to her bed. "My destiny is finished. Yours is about to begin. Your life lies before you like a beautiful river. It is nearly time for you to return and claim your rightful position as king in Mali. Your destiny is not here. Remember we had to run away like thieves in the night because of Sassouma and her son Dankaran. That is where you must take up the challenge. Better death than shame! Never forget that, my son."

"I shall never forget that, my mother!"

Part Eight: Sumangaru - The Sorcerer King

While Sundiata was away from his homeland, all the lands of the savanna had fallen under the domination of Sumangaru - the invincible King of Sosso. After defeating the kings of Ghana, no one dared oppose him anymore.

Sumangaru was descended from the line of blacksmiths who first harnessed fire and taught men to work with iron. And like all masters of fire, Sumangaru was a great sorcerer.

Sumangaru had fortified the town of Sosso with three walls. In the middle of the town was his palace with a seven-story tower that loomed over the thatched huts. He had terrible powers and all kings trembled before him. He could deal a swift death to whomever he pleased. Sumangaru felt that he was untouchable, and indeed, no man had the power of this sorcerer king! He was invulnerable to arrows. They bounced right off of him! In war he had never known defeat.

Years before, Sassouma and Dankaran had tried to keep their kingdom safe from Sumangaru. They had sent Balla Faseke, Sundiata's jali, to stay in Sumangaru's palace. And Sassouma had sent her own daughter, the beautiful Nana, to him as a bride. They had hoped these gifts of Nana and Balla Faseke would buy them peace.

But Sumangaru recognized that young king's weakness and easily conquered his land. Rather than fight, the cowardly Dankaran scampered off into the neighboring forests taking his mother with him. The people of Mali were without a leader.

And what had become of Nana and Balla Faseke? They knew of their people's suffering, but bided their time. They lived in Sosso in the palace of Sumangaru.

Even though the king had three hundred wives, Nana had become his favorite. She knew that she must become close to the king in order to learn of his powers. Balla Faseke had also earned the king's respect because of his good advice and wisdom. And so, they waited...

One day when the king was away, Balla Faseke snuck into the most secret chamber of the palace tower. He was amazed at what he saw.

On the walls were human skins stretched like trophies, and one covered Sumangaru's throne in the middle of the room. Nine human heads formed a circle around a huge sacrificial clay jar filled with water. There was evidence of blood and knives, and the room was full of idols. Perched above the bed were two guardian owls with their eyes partially open, sleepily observing the intruder at the door.

As Balla Faseke entered, a huge yellow and white snake lifted its head from the water in the jar. Balla, who was also a master of sorcery, recited magic incantations and the snake safely slid back under the water.

So frightened was Balla Faseke from the horrors of the chamber that he tried to scream, but no sound came from his throat. To keep from shaking, he called out a magic spell and his terror suddenly vanished. It was at that moment that he saw a large balafon - his favorite musical instrument, one in which he had been trained and over which he had special powers. The balafon before him was the balafon which the blacksmith and powerful sorcerer king Sumangaru played after each of his victories to accompany his own songs of praise for himself.

Balla could not help feel a surge of joy. He sat down to play a few notes with the little mallets. The wooden bars produced an extraordinary melody and harmony at the slightest touch. As he played, the guardian owls opened their eyes and moved their heads at the sweet sounds. The nine death heads began to come to life again. Yes! All those heads began to open their eyelids and lifted their lips in smiles.

Even though Sumangaru was absent from his palace in Sosso, he was mystically in touch with the balafon's spirit. He knew that someone had come into his most private chamber.

Furious, he dashed back to his palace and ran up the steps of the high tower. He rushed in the room with his sword drawn, shouting.

"It is I, Balla Faseke," the jali calmly replied. Then he began to play in honor of the king and his voice rang out in praise. The room filled with the magically sweet sounds.

The king was flattered by the praises and captivated by the music. (Did he not share the weaknesses of all men?) Sumangaru said, "I shall never touch the balafon again. From now on, you shall be my jali and it shall be your duty to play on this instrument after each of my victories."

In this way Sumangaru stole Sundiata's jali. War became inevitable.

Part Nine: Searching for Sundiata

Back in Mali, soothsayers whispered that the rightful heir would save them from their suffering under Sumangaru's rule. But where was the one who fled with his mother, brother, and sister many years before. Some of the elders secretly sent out search parties to find Sundiata, son of the Buffalo Woman. But where could he be found after these six years?

Sundiata was now strong enough to fight his enemies. At the age of eighteen he had distinguished himself in the army of the King of Mema and had a loyal following of young warriors.

One day Sundiata's younger sister went to the marketplace in Mema to buy some vegetables. There she saw a woman selling baobab leaves and vegetables from Mali. "How strange," the sister thought. "We have never seen these vegetables this far from home."

She spoke with the vegetable peddler. "It has been so long since we have seen vegetables like these from Mali. I will buy some for our mother, Sogolon, who is ill."

The peddler said, "Thanks to Allah that we have found Sogolon and her children. Our journey is not in vain. Please let us speak to your mother."

That night the search party came to Sogolon and Sundiata. "Alas! We bring you sad news. Sumangaru, the powerful king of Sosso, has heaped death and destruction upon Mali. The king, Dankaran, has fled and Mali is without a master. But the war is not finished yet. Warriors are waiting in the bush for a leader to return. Mali is saved because we have found you, Sundiata. The throne of your father awaits you. You are the cyclone that shall sweep the tyrant Sumangaru from the savanna forever."

Sogolon was overjoyed that her son was being called upon to greatness. She knew that the end of her mission in life coincided with the beginning of Sundiata's. That night the great woman who had nurtured Sundiata died.

Part Ten: The Return

The king was furious that Sundiata planned to leave Mema. After all, he hoped that Sundiata would be his heir, the next king. How ungrateful he thought Sundiata was. In anger he said, "You cannot leave here until you pay for the land to bury your mother in. If you cannot pay, you will have to take your mother's corpse with you!"

Sundiata eyes flamed. "Then I shall get the payment," he said and stalked out of the palace. Moments later he returned with an armload of broken calabashes, sand, pieces of pottery and other debris. "This is your payment," he said. And Sundiata went to get ready for his mother's burial.

"What does this mean?" the king asked his advisor. "How can this be payment for my land? Has Sundiata lost his mind?"

"It means that if you don't let him bury his mother and go with peace between you, the value of your land will be only this. He will destroy your kingdom. It will be where desert birds come to bathe in the dust."

The king was afraid, and he finally realized that Sundiata must go and fulfill his destiny. He gave in to Sundiata's wishes and held a great burial to honor his mother Sogolon. Then the king gave half of his own army to Sundiata. "We shall always be at peace, your kingdom and mine. I wished that you might be my successor. But this adopted home is not your own. May Allah be with you on your return."

With a small but well-trained cavalry dressed in Muslim outfits, Sundiata set out to confront Sumangaru's forces. He wore a white turban and a long cape. He rode a magnificent horse at the head of his cavalry. The war drums sounded as they left Mema. The soldiers carried their lances and swords. A troupe of archers followed them. But altogether they still were small in number. The people of Mema cheered them as they left and wished them well.

Sundiata's younger brother Manding Bory rode with him. "Can we hope to win with such a small army, my brother?"

"Numbers mean nothing, it is worth that counts. No matter how small a forest may be, you can always find there enough vines to tie up a man. I shall clear myself a path to Mali." And off they rode.

Not long after they crossed the border they came across an army led by one of Sumangaru's sons. Sundiata prepared to attack that very day. The orders were given and the war drums began to beat. On his horse Sundiata paraded in front of his troops and encouraged them. Then he led the charge, shouting his war cry.

APPENDIX D

The soldiers of Sosso were surprised by this sudden attack. They expected the battle to begin the next day. The lightning that flashes across the sky is slower than Sundiata's swooping down on the warriors of Sosso. Sundiata was in their midst like a lion among its prey. All around him Sosso warriors fell from his sword as ripe fruit falls from a shaken tree. And the son of Sumangaru turned in flight to report to his father about the defeat at the hands of Sundiata.

The army of Mali celebrated their first victory.

News of the victory and of Sundiata's triumphal return to the savanna spread as if carried by the wind. Sons of Mali rallied to him and pledged their loyalty.

Next they were joined by the army of Tabon. Sundiata was greeted by his friend Fran who said, "I renew my oath to you made many years ago. I pledge myself to conquer or to die by your side. We will free ourselves from the tyrant of Sosso!" The warriors of Mema, Tabon, and Mali shouted their approval becoming one great army united in purpose.

Other brave princes came to pledge their loyalty to Sundiata. They performed great feats of strength and bravery, and were welcomed under Sundiata's command!

All the rebel princes who came to Sundiata were still in their youth - a time when a human bursts into life like the most brilliant meteor, with bravery, enthusiasm and dedication - a meteor that loses its radiance with age.

Within days, Sumangaru marched out to meet Sundiata. As usual, the son of Sogolon wanted to battle right away. The king of Sosso drew his men across a narrow valley with his troops on the slopes of the hills. Sundiata formed his cavalry in a tight square leading the attack, with his archers at the back. Sumangaru was perched high on a hill. He could be recognized by his helmet with many horns.

The trumpets, drums, and balafons sounded and encouraged the warriors. Soon the valley disappeared in a cloud of red dust kicked up by thousands of feet and hooves. Without giving an inch, the forces of Sumangaru stopped the wave of attack.

Sumangaru gave a signal from the hill to blacksmith warriors to swoop down into the valley to encircle Sundiata. Without a word, Sundiata's square of soldiers extended themselves into a rectangle. Everything had been foreseen. The change was so quick that Sumangaru's men halted and could not use their weapons. From the rear, the archers began their task. Arrows fell on Sumangaru's forces like a rain of iron. The forces of Mali continued the attack with new strength.

Sumangaru was still perched high on the hill. Sundiata left his soldiers behind and alone he charged toward his enemy. He shot an arrow at the sorcerer king, but Sumangaru grabbed it in mid-air. He raised the arrow, waved it, and laughed. Then Sundiata threw his metal spear, but that only bounced off Sumangaru's chest. "Ha, Sundiata! I am invincible."

Then Sumangaru disappeared! A moment later he was across the valley on another hill. Sundiata could hear his taunting laughter echoing down the valley.

He reappeared closer to Sundiata. "Know that I have already killed nine kings whose heads adorn my room. Yours shall be put next to theirs. Prepare yourself for your death!" Then he disappeared again before Sundiata's eyes.

Sundiata was amazed at the power of the sorcerer king. "How can I defeat a man who can disappear and reappear where and when he likes? How can I conquer a man invulnerable to my iron spear and to my arrows? Clearly other weapons are necessary."

As the sun was setting, Sundiata was master of the valley. And as others began to celebrate their victory, he could only wonder, "How was Sumangaru able to escape me? Why is he invulnerable to my weapons? What is the secret of his power?"

Part Eleven: The Secret of Sumangaru

Nana was Sundiata's half-sister and she had grown up to have all the beauty that both her father and her mother were known for. Sundiata had always been a loving brother to her. Nana shared none of the hatred or jealousy that her own mother and brother had for Sundiata. When her own brother Dankaran sent her to be the wife of Sumangaru, at first she was angry. But when she saw the suffering of her people, she decided that she may be in a position to find the secret of the king's invulnerability.

Sumangaru had three hundred wives, but because of her beauty, Nana became his favorite. Through beauty and guile, she gained a closeness and a power over the king. She moved around easily in her web of lies - as at home in flattery and deceit as a fish in water. She would try to catch Sumangaru at his own game.

One evening she went up to his tower room. She offered him wine and her legendary beauty inspired him. "Drink, my love. There is plenty of honey in it, my sweet king," she said.

Sumangaru was in a confident mood and he was eager to hear more compliments.

"Oooh, don't look into my eyes, for no woman can bear the brilliance of your gaze," she sighed. "You are the light of my sky."

Next Nana turned away, but not so much as to let her tears go unnoticed.

"Why are you crying?" he asked.

"I am crying because I am afraid you will abandon me one day. I love you so and I can't live without you! Will you ever send me away?"

"No, my love." And he raised his cup once again to his lips.

"You are such a great man. Tell me if there is anything I should not do in case it might diminish your magnificent powers?" Nana had cast her web and waited for what it would bring.

"Don't worry," he smiled. "I can only be hurt by the spur from the foot of a white rooster."

"I am so lucky to have you near me. And I will take good care of all that you have told me," she said as she smiled and put her head on his shoulder.

Part Twelve: The Battle of Kirina

Sumangaru's main camp was several days' march to the north on the broad plains of Kirina.

As Sundiata and his army advanced to Kirina, more sons of Mali joined him. He gave the people hope that at last the powerful sorcerer king could be defeated and that Sumangaru's kingdom would collapse under him like a horse worn out beneath its rider. Then they would be free.

Two days before the battle, two mysterious visitors came riding up to Sundiata. In disguise were Nana, his half-sister, and his jali, Balla Faseke. "My brother," Nana greeted him. "We have escaped from Sosso and now join you. I am your sister and this is Balla, your jali, returned to you."

"Is this Nana?" he asked. "You have grown so. And Balla, I have missed your advice and friendship as I grew. You both belong by my side!"

Sundiata saw Nana's eyes were bathed in tears, so great was her joy at their reunion. "Oh, my brother. You know that I never wanted you to leave Mali. It was my mother who did all that. I too was sent out. Now our homeland is destroyed, its inhabitants scattered. Many of our people have been carried off into captivity."

"Do not cry, Nana," said Sundiata. "What happened was not your fault. Everything that has happened was destined. It was good for me to spend some years in exile. Exile inspires wisdom."

"But Nana, tell him what you have learned," urged Balla Faseke impatiently.

"My brother," Nana said. "I must warn you that the evil king cannot be defeated by your arrows or your spears. But know what I have learned... His magic can only be destroyed by the spur of a white rooster. Here," she said as she handed him an arrow she had prepared. "This will bring you victory."

"So that is his secret. Mali will always be grateful to you, my sister." And he accepted the arrow with increased confidence.

On the eve of the battle, Sundiata ordered the slaughter of oxen to supply a great feast to his soldiers. But while the feast filled their bellies, the soldiers were apprehensive before this great conflict in which many would die.

Balla Faseke said, "Let me talk to the men. Let my words fill their hearts." And so he began as they gathered around the great campfires:

"Kingdoms and empires have lifetimes like man. They too are born, grow, and disappear. Today a new kingdom rises as one dies. Sosso was the growth of yesterday, whereas Mali is for tomorrow." He reminded them of their great heritage and told of their glorious future. He praised each of the kings who joined forces with Mali. And he told them of the prophecy of their leader, their general - the son of the buffalo, lion, and panther - who would rule the savanna. Then he concluded:

"But these are just words: power lies in deeds. Be men of action. Do not respond with your voice, but tomorrow carry out the deeds that will bring fame and glory to you and your ancestors."

After Balla had inflamed their fighting spirit, each went to rest or to prepare for the morning's task without fear.

Sundiata was alone outside his tent as the moon rose. He heard the flapping of wings and saw an owl perch on a nearby branch. It was one of the owls that Balla Faseke had seen in the chamber of the Sumangaru's tower and it was sent as a messenger. Here is the dialog between Sundiata and Sumangaru relayed by the sorcerer-bird:

Owl: "Behave yourself, little boy. I am the king of Mali. If you want peace, return to Mema."
Sundiata: "I will achieve my destiny here in Mali. It is you who will leave."
Owl: "I am the wild yam of the rocks; nothing will make me leave Mali."
Sundiata: "I have master smiths who will shatter the rocks. Then, yam, I will devour you."
Owl: "I am the red-hot cinder on which you will burn the soles of your feet!"
Sundiata: "I am the rain that will extinguish the cinder and wash it away."

Then Sundiata grew tired of the battle with words. "Diabolical little bird, go and tell your master that I wish no further speech with him. I am not a jali, I am a man of action. Tomorrow I shall wage war."

The owl flew away into the darkness.

When left alone, Sundiata walked further out onto the plains. There he heard the sounds of animals. He heard the roar of a lion, the snarl of a panther, and the bellowing of a buffalo. Before the battle, other rebel princes heard or saw their guardian spirits, too. Balla Faseke saw the hawk. Another the eagle. Another a snake. The totem animals were gathering to give power to the young warriors.

At first light the two great armies gathered facing each other across the plain. The drums sounded and the battle began. Sundiata's cavalry charged as his archers shot a barrage of arrows.

APPENDIX D

Sundiata's full army advanced. Swords clashed, hoof beats pounded, and war drums thundered. The battle was in full swing.

Sundiata saw Sumangaru at the crest of a hill. Raising his bow, he shot the arrow fixed with the spur of a white rooster. The arrow flew straight but only grazed his shoulder. Immediately Sumangaru felt his powers leave him. Trembling, he let out a great cry. He looked up toward the sun. A great black bird flew over the battle field and he understood. It was the bird of misfortune. "The bird of Kirina," he muttered. He turned his horse's head and took flight.

The forces of Sumangaru saw their king leave, and they fled in turn. It was a complete victory for Sundiata. Death hovered over the great plain and blood poured out of a thousand wounds.

Sundiata pursued Sumangaru on horseback up a mountain. He wanted to catch him alive. Throwing his spear, he made Sumangaru's horse fall. The old king picked himself up. Then a wild chase began on foot. Before him appeared a gaping cave which seemed to draw him against his will. Sundiata's footsteps sounded close behind. Sumangaru entered the black cave where he disappeared into the mountain. Sundiata could not find him, and he shouted, "Come out, coward!"

A loud "Never!" echoed through the darkness. In spite of his search, Sundiata found no trace of his enemy. He mounted his horse and turned back down the mountain.

Sundiata returned to the battle field. His forces had been completely victorious. His troops were rejoicing in their spectacular success.

Days later Sundiata laid siege to Sosso, the spectacular city of the sorcerer king. The drums sounded and the tide of soldiers moved forward. Warriors with swords, spears and shields were in the first line. Warriors with ladders were in the second. The main body attacked the single city gate with flaming arrows and battering rams. The city was completely taken in a short time.

Sundiata was now in front of the awesome palace tower. Balla Faseke, who knew every inch of the palace, led him into the king's magic chamber. It had changed its appearance since the sorcerer had lost his power. The snake was writhing in pains of death. Two owls were flapping pitifully on the floor.

Sumangaru's seven-story tower with all its idols was then burned and Sosso was destroyed completely. It is now a place where only birds come to take their dust baths.

As Sundiata and his army made their triumphal march back to his homeland, the festivals began. There was great rejoicing. The Lion King Sundiata was proclaimed emperor by the twelve kings of the savanna. Twelve royal spears were stuck in the ground as a pledge to unity.

This is the story of the Lion King, Sundiata, my children. Don't doubt my words. I teach you of our time of greatness. The past is only the seed of the future.

APPENDIX E

Recommended Resources

Europe in the Middle Ages

Gardner, John. *Grendal.* Vintage, 1989. (The *Beowulf* epic from Grendal's point of view.)

Sutcliff, Rosemary. *The Shining Company.* Farrar, Straus, and Giroux, 1990 (Historic Fiction. 7th century Britain's battle with the invading Saxons)

Cushman, Karen. *Matilda Bone.* New York: Clarion Books, 2000.

Nardo, Don. *Life on a Medieval Pilgrimage.* San Diago, CA: Lucent Books, 1998

Garden, Nancy. *Dove and Sword: A Novel of Joan of Arc.* New York: Farrar, Straus, & Giroux, 1995.

McCaughrean, Geraldine. *El Cid.* Oxford University Press, 1988.

Hinds, Katherine. *Medieval England.* Benchmark Books, 2002.

Leaon, Vicki. *Outrageous Women in the Middle Ages.* Wiley, 1998.

Henty, G.A. *Wulf the Saxon.* Retold by Jim Weiss on audio CD. PrestonSpeed Publications, 2001. (The story of the Norman Conquest and the Battle of Hastings in 1066.)

Pyle, Howard. *Men of Iron.* Mineola, New York: Dover Publications, 2003. (Historic fiction. A young boy trains to be a knight in 15th century England.)

Picard, Barbara Leonie. *Tales of the Norse Gods.* Oxford: Oxford University Press, 2001.

Leighton, Margaret. *Twelve Bright Trumpets.* Centerville, VA: AHSP, 2004. (Twelve historic fiction stories that span the Middle Ages from the fall of Rome to the fall of Venice.)

French, Allen. *The Story of Rolf and the Viking Bow.* Bathgate, ND: Bethlehem Books, 1994.

French, Allen. *The Red Keep.* Bathgate, ND: Bethlehem Books, 1997. (Historic fiction. 13th century Europe during the 2nd crusade.)

Sutcliff, Rosemary. *The Latern Bearers.* Farrar, Straus, and Giroux, 1994. (Historic Fiction. The last Roman Auxiliaries are leaving Britain but one young legionnaire stays behind.)

Tolkien, J.R.R. *Sir Gawain and the Green Knight*, *Pearl,* and *Sir Orfeo.* New York: Ballantine Books, 1975.

Jewett, Eleanore M. *The Hidden Treasure of Galston.* Bathgate, ND: Bethlehem Books, 2000.

Sutcliff, Rosemary. *Sword Song.* Farrar, Straus, and Giroux, 1994. (Historic fiction. A young Viking swordsman is banished from his home.)

Welch, Ronald. *The Gauntlet.* Oxford: Oxford University Press, 1999. (Peter travels back in time to 14th century Europe during the time of castles, hawking, and battles.)

Jackdaw Portfolios. *The Black Death.* Amawalk, N.Y.: Jackdaw Publications.

Jackdaw Portfolios. *1066.* Amawalk, N.Y.: Jackdaw Publications.

Asia

Barrett, Tracy. *Anna of Byzantium.* New York: Delacorte Press, 1999.

Walsh, Jill Paton. *The Emperor's Winding Sheet.* Ashville, North Carolina: Front Street, 1974. (Historic Fiction. The story of the fall of Constantinople and the end of the Byzantine Empire.)

Stanley, Diane. *Saladin, Noble Prince of Islam.* New York: HarperCollins, 2002. (Beautifully illustrated book about the crusades from a Muslim point of view.)

Greenblatt, Miriam. *Genghis Khan and the Mongol Empire.* New York: Benchmark Books, 2001.

Butson, Thomas. *Ivan the Terrible.* New York: Chelsea House Publications, 1987.

Kimmel, Eric. *Sword of the Samurai : Adventure Stories from Japan.* New York: HarperTrophy, 2001.

Jackdaw Portfolios. *Byzantine Empire.* Amawalk, N.Y.: Jackdaw Publications.

Herbert, Janis. *Marco Polo for Kids.* Chicago: Chicago Review Press, 2001. (An informative activity book.)

Park, Linda Sue. *A Single Shard.* Yearling , 2003. (Historic fiction. A look at a craftsmen's colony from Medieval Korea.)

The Americas

Steele, Philip, ed. *The Aztec News.* Cambridge, MA: Candlewick Press, 1997.

Baquedano, Elizabeth, et al. *Aztec, Inca and Maya.* New York: Knopf, 1993.

Jackdaw Portfolios. *Incas: A Cultural History.* Amawalk, N.Y.: Jackdaw Publications.

Africa

Millar, Heather. *The Kingdom of Benin in West Africa.* New York: Benchmark Books, 1996.

McKissack, Patrick and Frederick. *The Royal Kingdoms of Ghana, Mali, and Songhay : Life in Medieval Africa.* Henry Holt and Co. , 1995.

Europe in the Renaissance

Meyer, Carolyn. *Beware, Princess Elizabeth.* New York: Gullivar Books, 2001. (Part of the *Young Royals* series. Tells the story of Elizabeth Tudor in her teenage years.)

Meyer, Carolyn. *Doomed Queen Anne.* New York: Gulliver Books, 2002. (Part of the *Young Royals* series.)

Meyer, Carolyn. *Mary, Bloody Mary.* New York: Gulliver Books, 2000. (Part of the *Young Royals* series.)

Meyer, Carolyn. *Patience, Princess Catherine.* New York: Gulliver Books, 2001. (Part of the *Young Royals* series.)

Lasky, Katheryn. *Elizabeth I, Red Rose of the House of Tudor.* New York: Scholastic, Inc. , 2002. (Part of *The Royal Diary* series.)

Lasky, Katheryn. *Mary, Queen of Scots, Queen Without a Country.* New York: Scholastic, Inc. , 2002. (Part of *The Royal Diary* series.)

Yolen, Jane and Harris, Robert J. *Queen's Own Fool, A Novel of Mary Queen of Scots.* New York: Penguin Group (USA) Inc. , 2000.

Columbus, Christopher. *First Voyage to America, From the Log of the "Santa Maria."* New York: Dover Publications, 1991.

Johansen, Joann. *Fine Print: A Story About Johann Gutenberg.* Carolrhoda Books, 1992.

Worksheets

Below is a list of the worksheets included with this course. You might want to make copies of all the worksheets, and not write on the original.

Elements of an Epic

Feudalism Chart

The Middle Ages Around the World

Medieval English Social Class Chart

Character Webs from The Canterbury Tales

My Character Web

Plot Diagram

The Maya, Aztec, and Inca Empire Characteristics

The Maya, Aztec, and Inca Empire Venn Diagram

The Renaissance Web

Henry VIII's Family Tree

The Tudor Family Reunion

The Renaissance Around the World

Timeline Analysis

Elements of an Epic

Title: _____

Determine if the story you read is an epic by searching for examples of each element in the story. Write the examples from the story on the chart.

Element	Example
The main character is a hero, who often possess supernatural abilities or qualities.	
The hero is charged with a quest.	
The hero is tested, often to prove the worthiness of himself and his quest.	
The presence of numerous mythical beings, magical and helpful animals, and /or human helpers.	
The hero's travels take him to a supernatural world, often one that normal beings are barred from entering.	
The cycle must reach a low point where the hero nearly gives up his quest or appears defeated.	
A resurrection occurs where the hero resumes his quest.	
Restitution. Often takes the form of the hero regaining his rightful place on the throne or in society.	

This chart was modified and reproduced with permission by the National Endowment for the Humanities as part of the Marco Polo Project. The online lesson can be found at http://edsitement.neh.gov/view_lesson_plan.asp?id=587.

Feudalism Chart

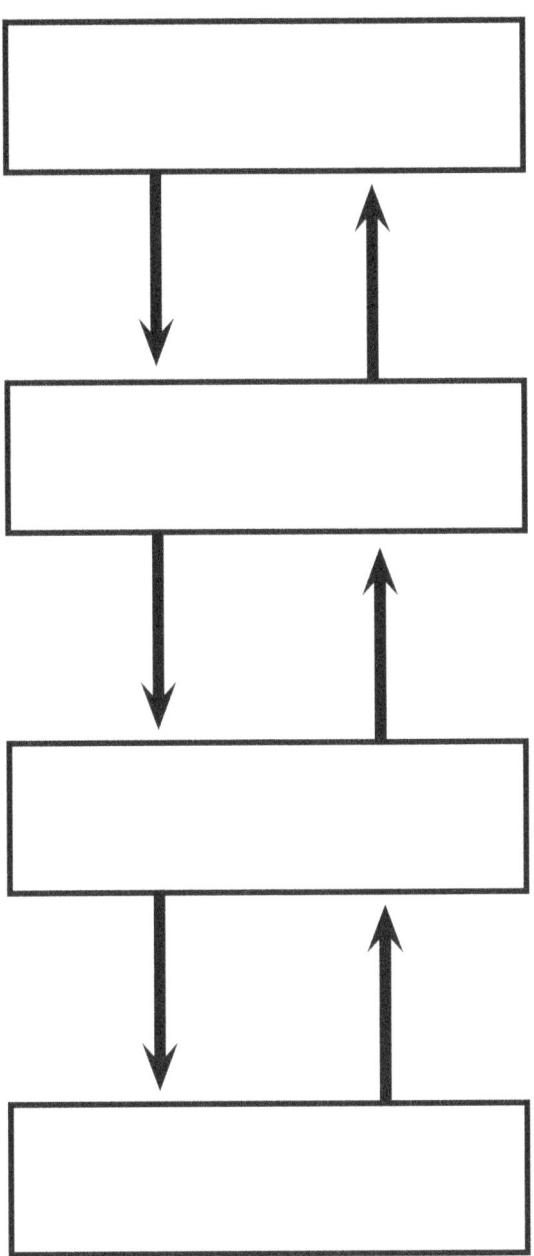

Summary of the Feudal System:

The Middle Ages Around the World
500 - 1460

Russia

Korea

China

Japan

India

Middle East

Africa

The Americas

Italy

England

Spain

France

Medieval English Social Class Chart

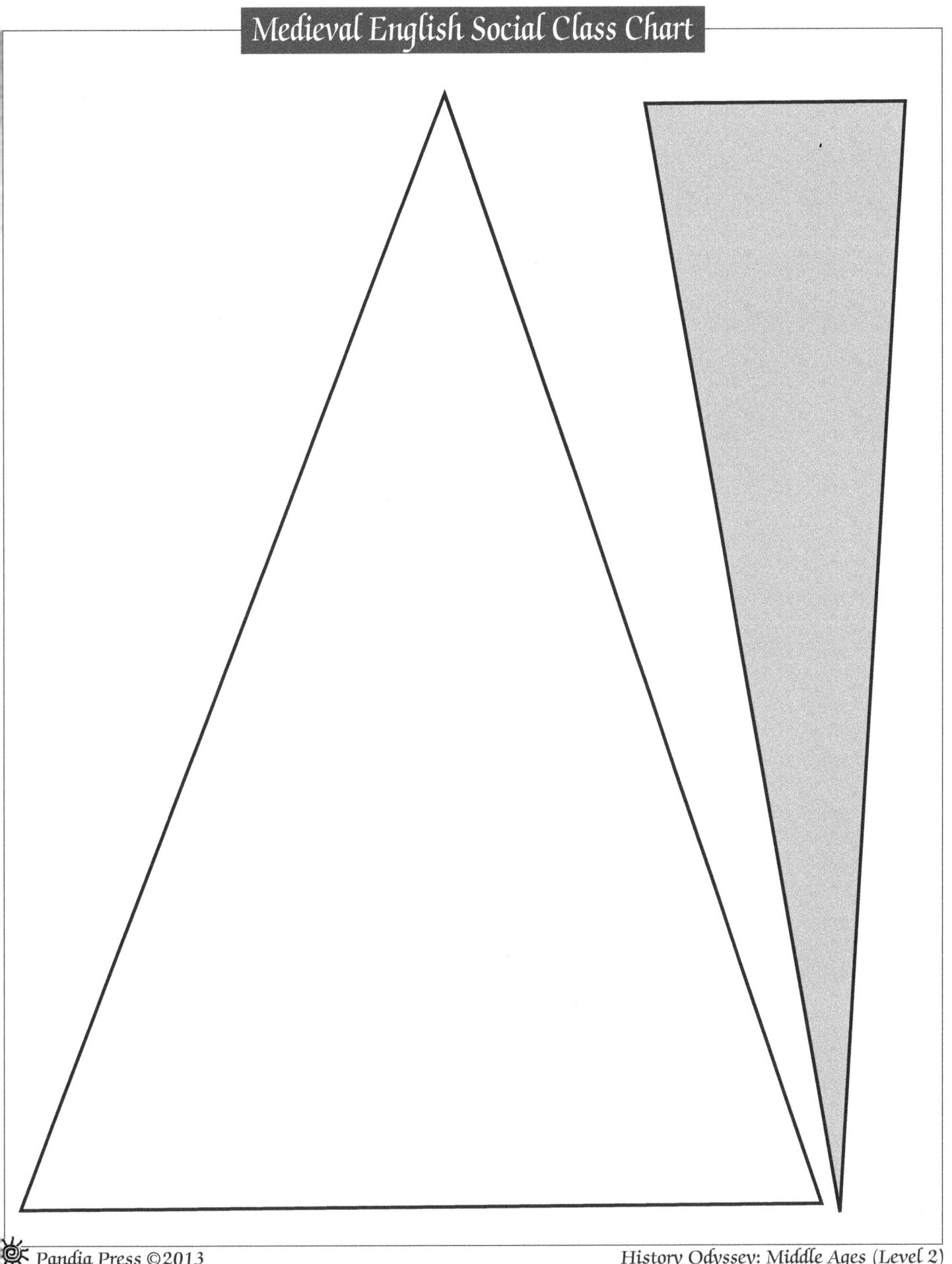

Character Webs from The Canterbury Tales

Write the name of the character in the center circle. Write characteristics and descriptions of the character in the surrounding circles.

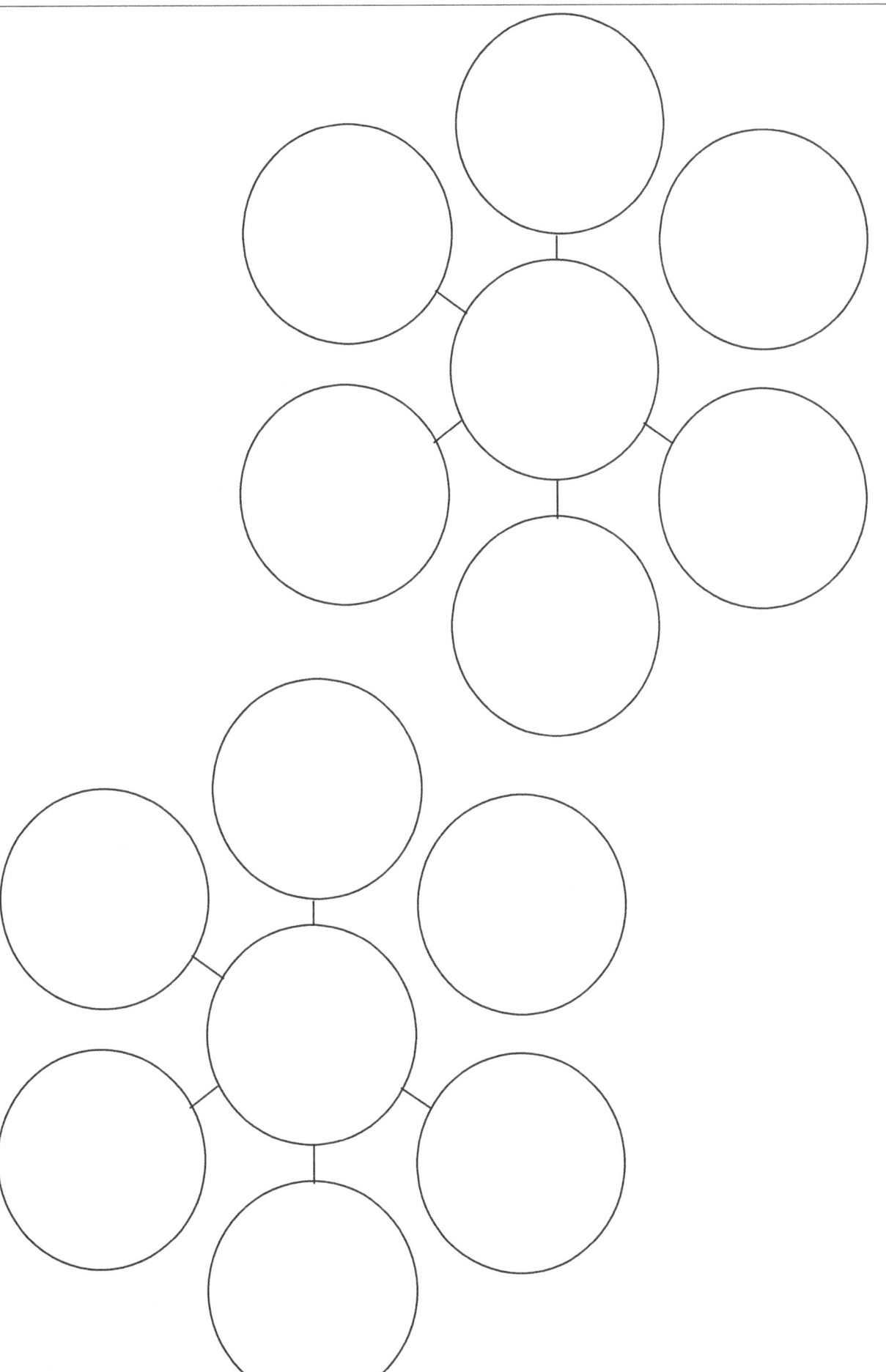

History Odyssey: Middle Ages (Level 2)

Pandia Press ©2013

My Character Web

Plot Diagram

Title: _____

Write the protagonist and the antagonist of the story. Then fill in the events from the story in their proper place on the diagram. You can write on the diagram itself or use the boxes below.

Protagonist =

Antagonist =

Climax

Falling Action

Rising Action

Resolution

Exposition

Exposition	Rising Action	Climax	Falling Action	Resolution

History Odyssey: Middle Ages (Level 2)

Pandia Press ©2013

The Maya, Aztec, and Inca Empires Characteristics

	Maya	Aztec	Inca
Time Period			
Geographic Location			
Religion			
Farming			
Food			
Architecture			
Education			
Wars			
Clothing			
Politics/Government			
Occupations			
Leaders			
Downfall			

The Maya, Aztec, and Inca Empires Venn Diagram

The Inca Empire

The Aztec Empire

The Maya Empire

The Renaissance Web

- What
- When
- Who
- The Renaissance
- Where
- How
- Why

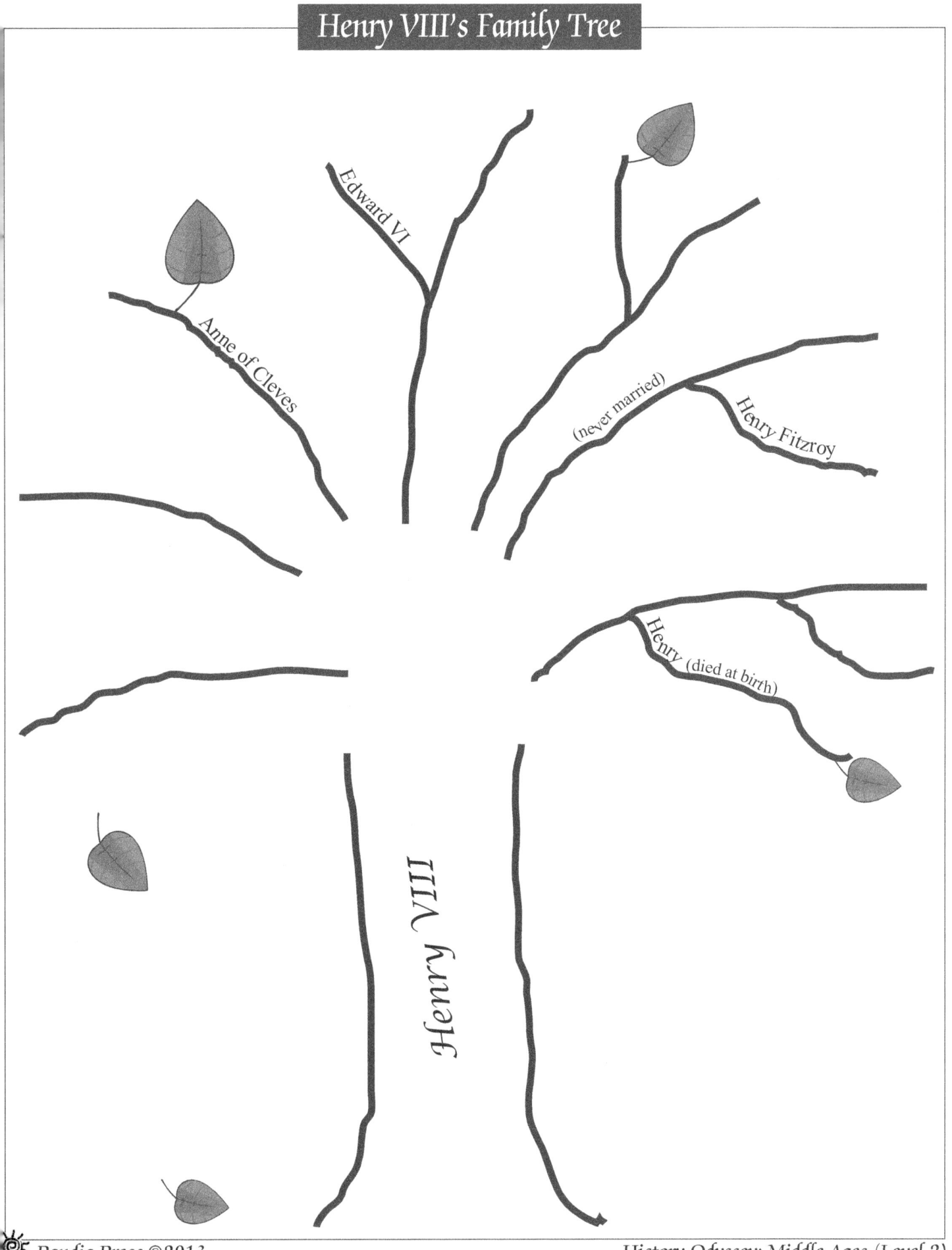

Tudor Family Reunion

You have been hired to assist the Tudors with their family reunion. The reunion should be interesting since many of the family members despise each other. Miraculously, even some of the deceased members will be making an appearance. Each family member must stand and make a short speech. Your job is to write their speeches. Each speech should describe the guest, include an important accomplishment, and communicate how the guest feels about the others present. Do your best work; you wouldn't want a Tudor upset with you!

Speech for Henry VIII

Speech for Catherine of Aragon

Speech for Anne Boleyn

Speech for Jane Seymour

Speech for Elizabeth I

Speech for Mary Tudor

Speech for _____

The Renaissance Around the World
1460 - 1600

- Russia
- Korea
- China
- Japan
- India
- Middle East
- Africa
- The Americas
- Italy
- England
- Spain
- France

Timeline Analysis

Area / Date range	Europe	The Middle East	Africa	East Asia	The Americas
500 - 600 (100 years)					
601 - 650 (50 years)					
651 - 700					
701 - 750					
751 - 800					
801 - 850					
851 - 900					

Timeline Analysis

Area / Date range	Europe	The Middle East	Africa	East Asia	The Americas
901 - 950					
951 - 1000					
1001 - 1050					
1051 - 1100					
1101 - 1150					
1151 - 1200					
1201 - 1250					

Timeline Analysis

Area / Date range	Europe	The Middle East	Africa	East Asia	The Americas
1251 - 1300					
1301 - 1350					
1351 - 1400					
1401 - 1450					
1451 - 1500					
1501 - 1550					
1551 - 1600					

Maps

Below is a list of the maps included with this course. You might want to make extra copies of the maps, saving the original.

Map 1   Barbarian Invasion
Map 2   The Diaspora
Map 3   The Empire of Charlemagne
Map 4   Medieval Europe
Map 5   The Viking World
Map 6   Norman Invasion
Map 7   The Holy Roman Empire
Map 8   The First Crusade
Map 9   Medieval Ireland
Map 10   European Medieval Trade Routes
Map 11   Medieval Explorers
Map 12   The Black Death
Map 13   The Hundred Years' War
Map 14   The Byzantine Empire
Map 15   The Islamic Empire
Map 16   Russian Expansion 1613
Map 17   Safavid Persia
Map 18   The Ottoman Empire
Map 19   Medieval China
Map 20   The Mongol Empire
Map 21   Mogul India
Map 22   Medieval Japan
Map 23   North America
Map 24   Central and South America
Map 25   African Kingdoms
Map 26   The Reunification of Spain
Map 27   The Portuguese and Spanish Empires
Map 28   European Explorers
Map 29   The Hapsburgs & The Netherlands

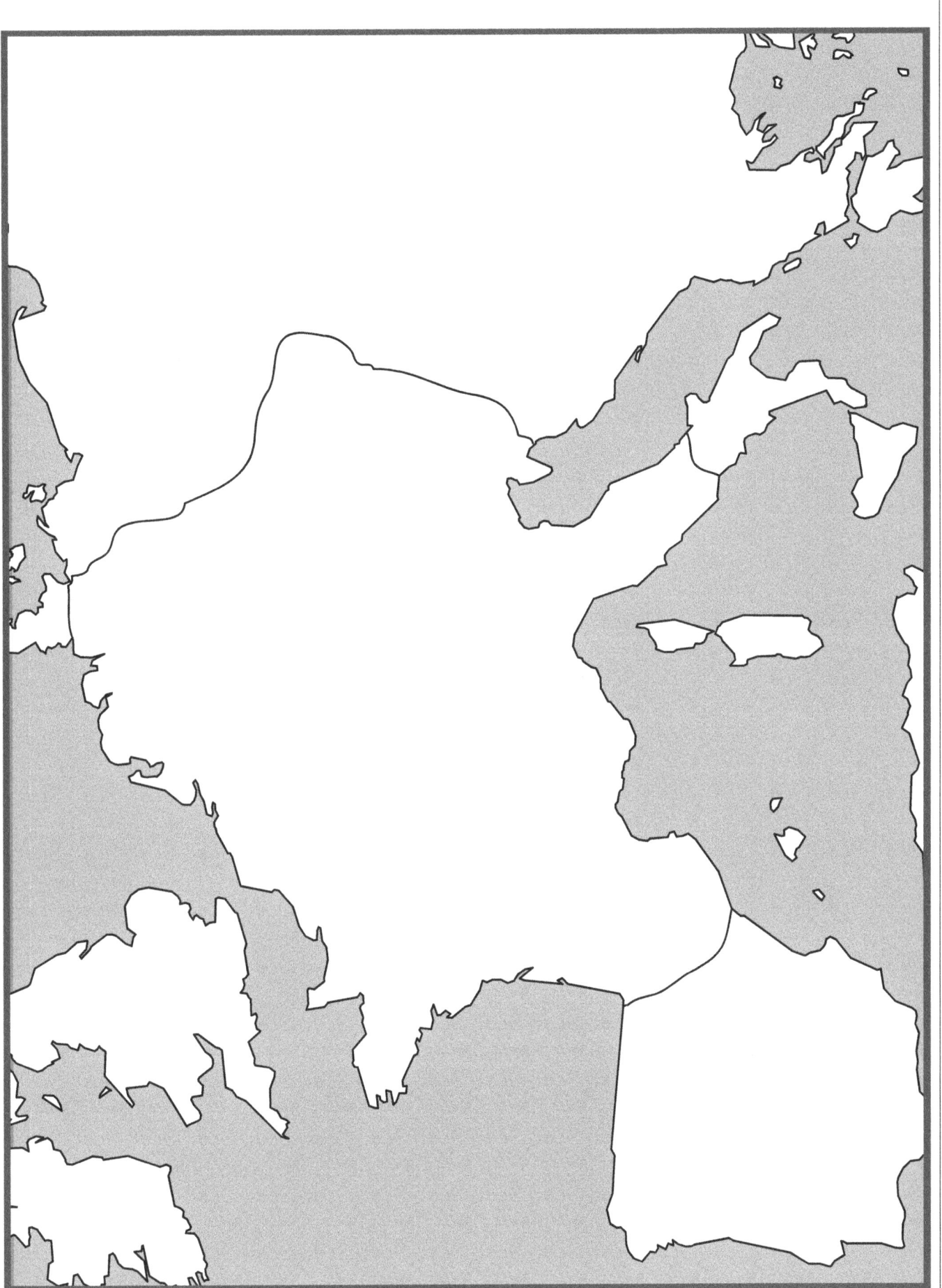

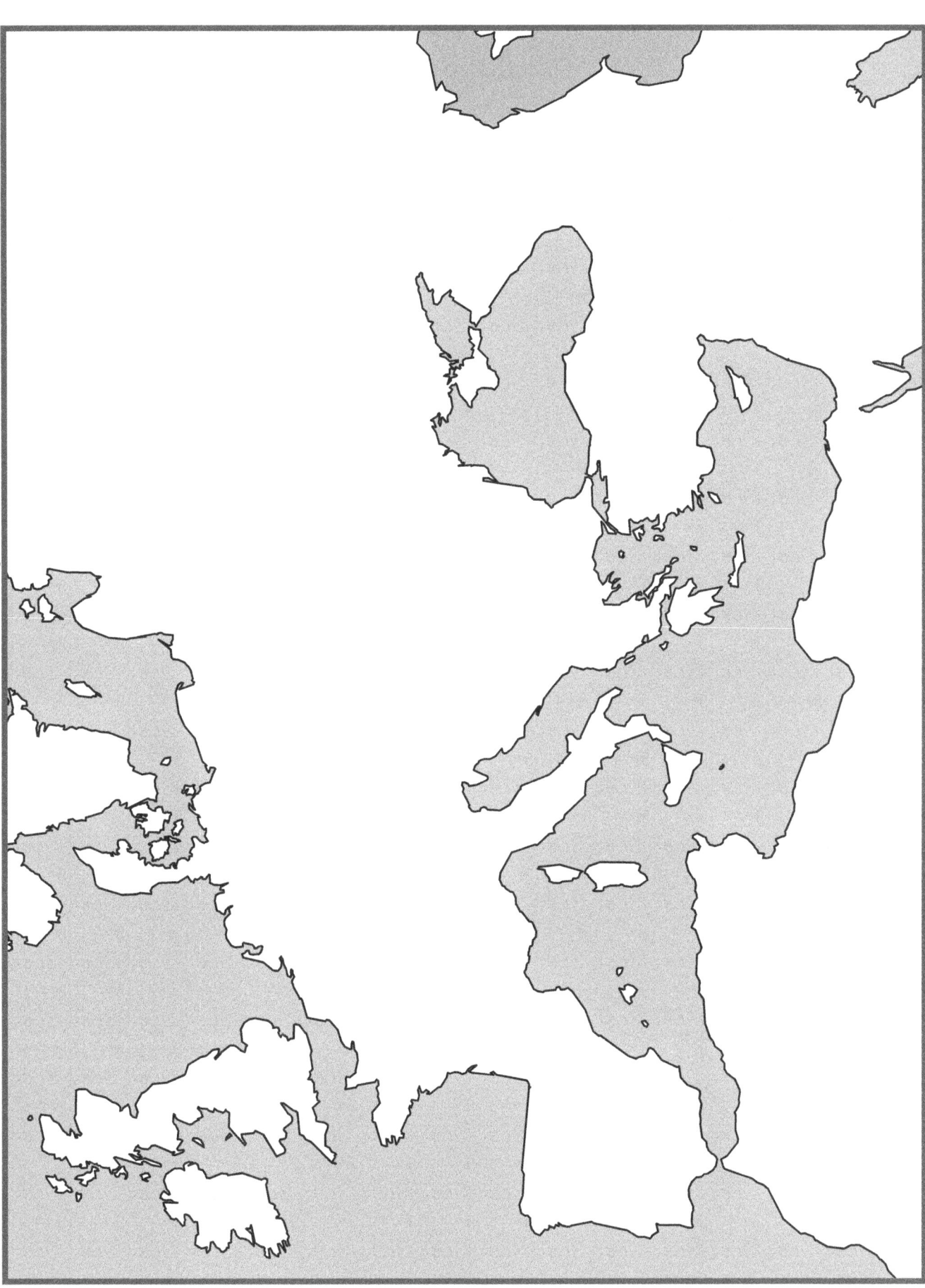

Medieval Europe

History Odyssey: Middle Ages (Level 2)

Pandia Press ©2013

Map 5

The Viking World

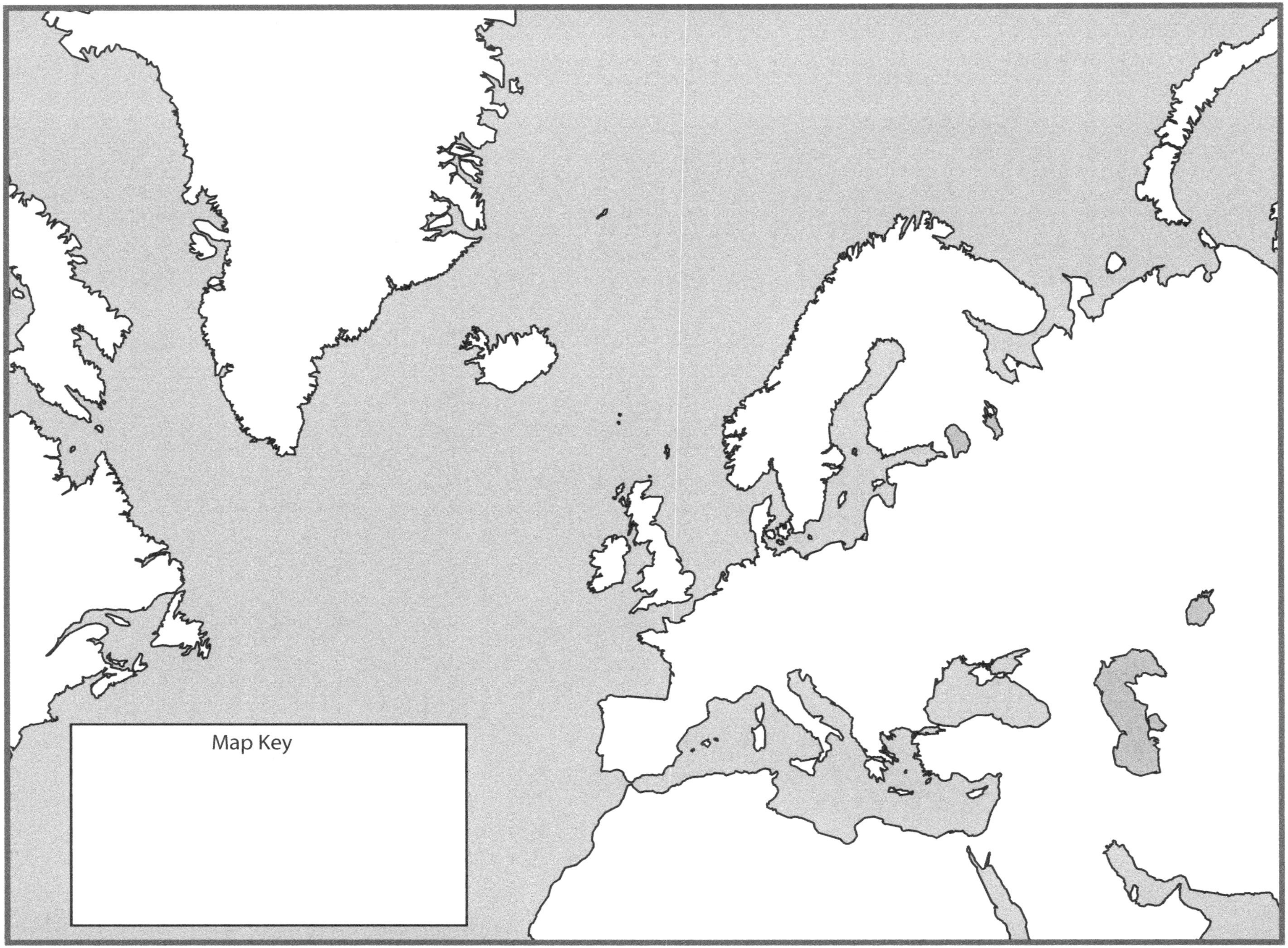

Map Key

History Odyssey: Middle Ages (Level 2)

Pandia Press ©2013

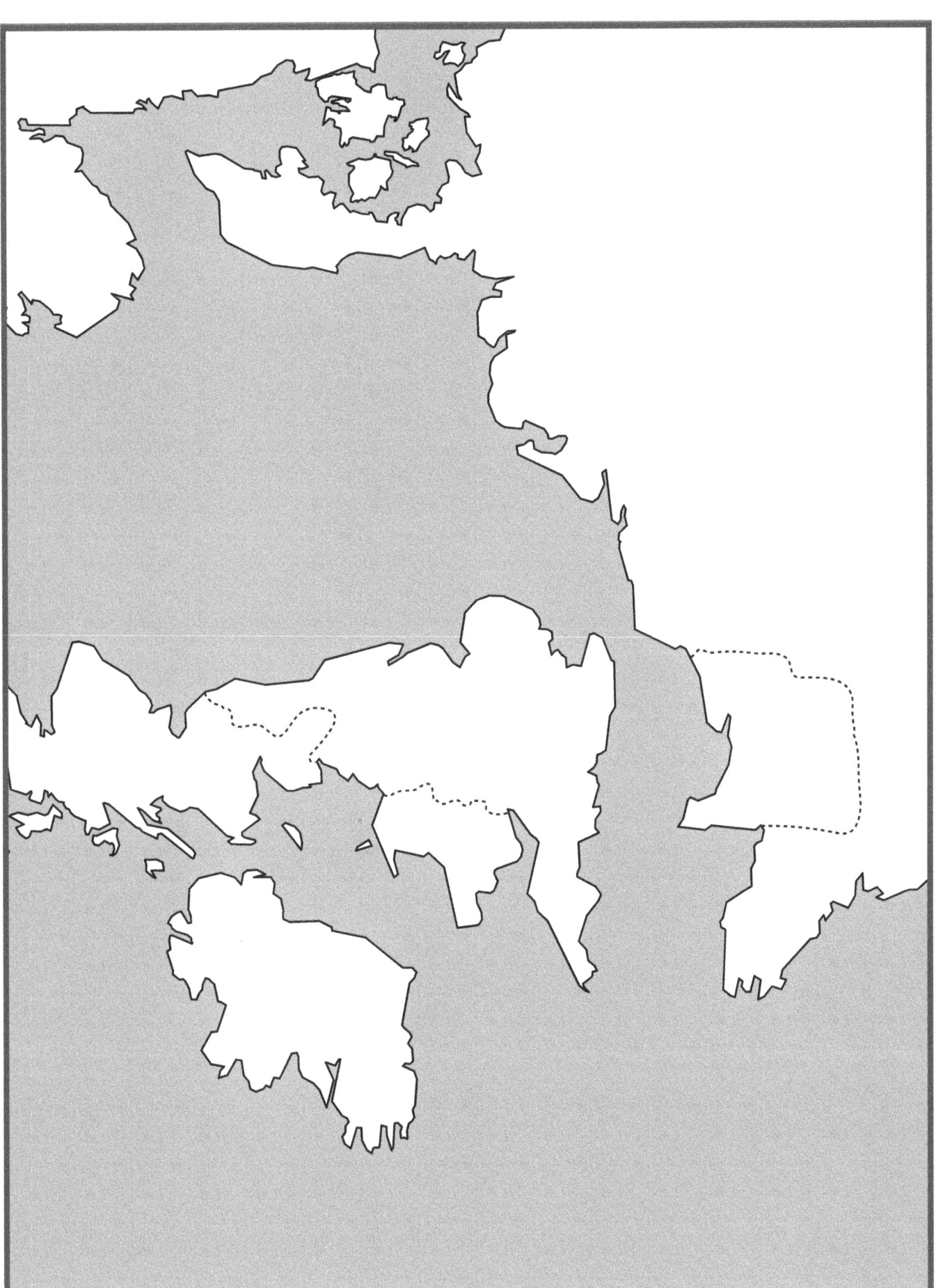

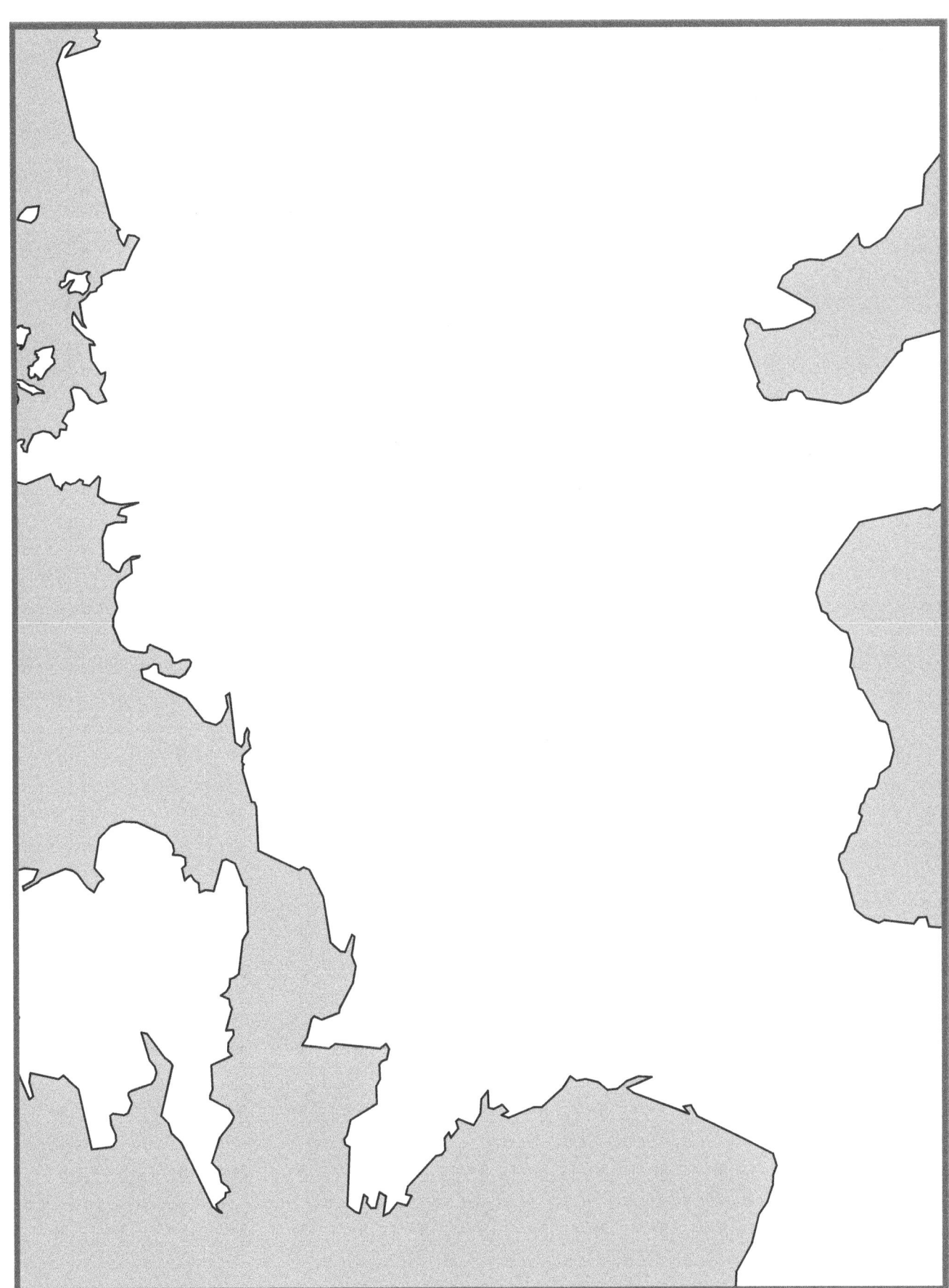

The Holy Roman Empire

History Odyssey: Middle Ages (Level 2) — Pandia Press ©2013

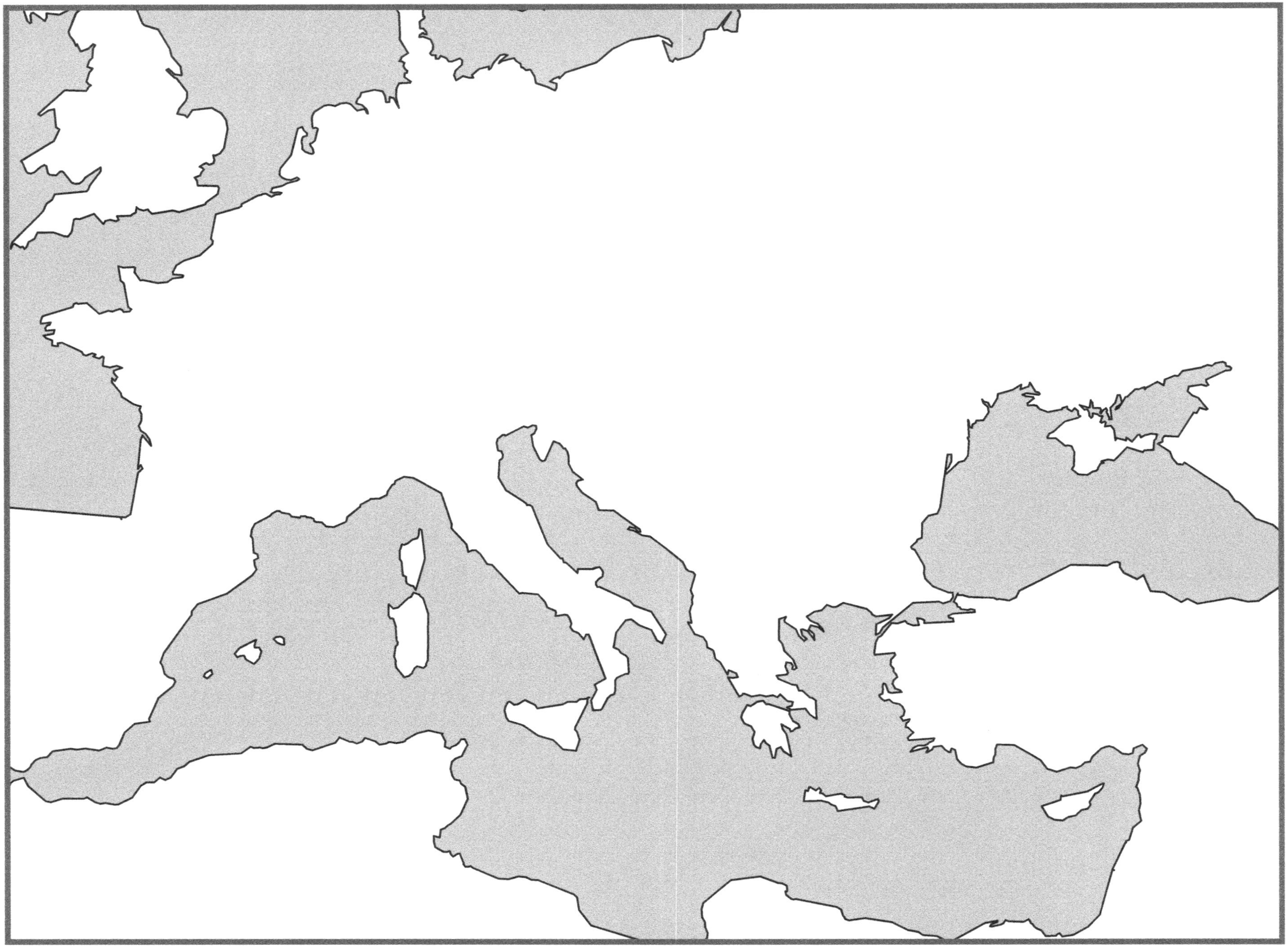

Map 8

The First Crusade

History Odyssey: Middle Ages (Level 2)

Pandia Press ©2013

Medieval Ireland

History Odyssey: Middle Ages (Level 2)

Pandia Press ©2013

European Medieval Trade Routes

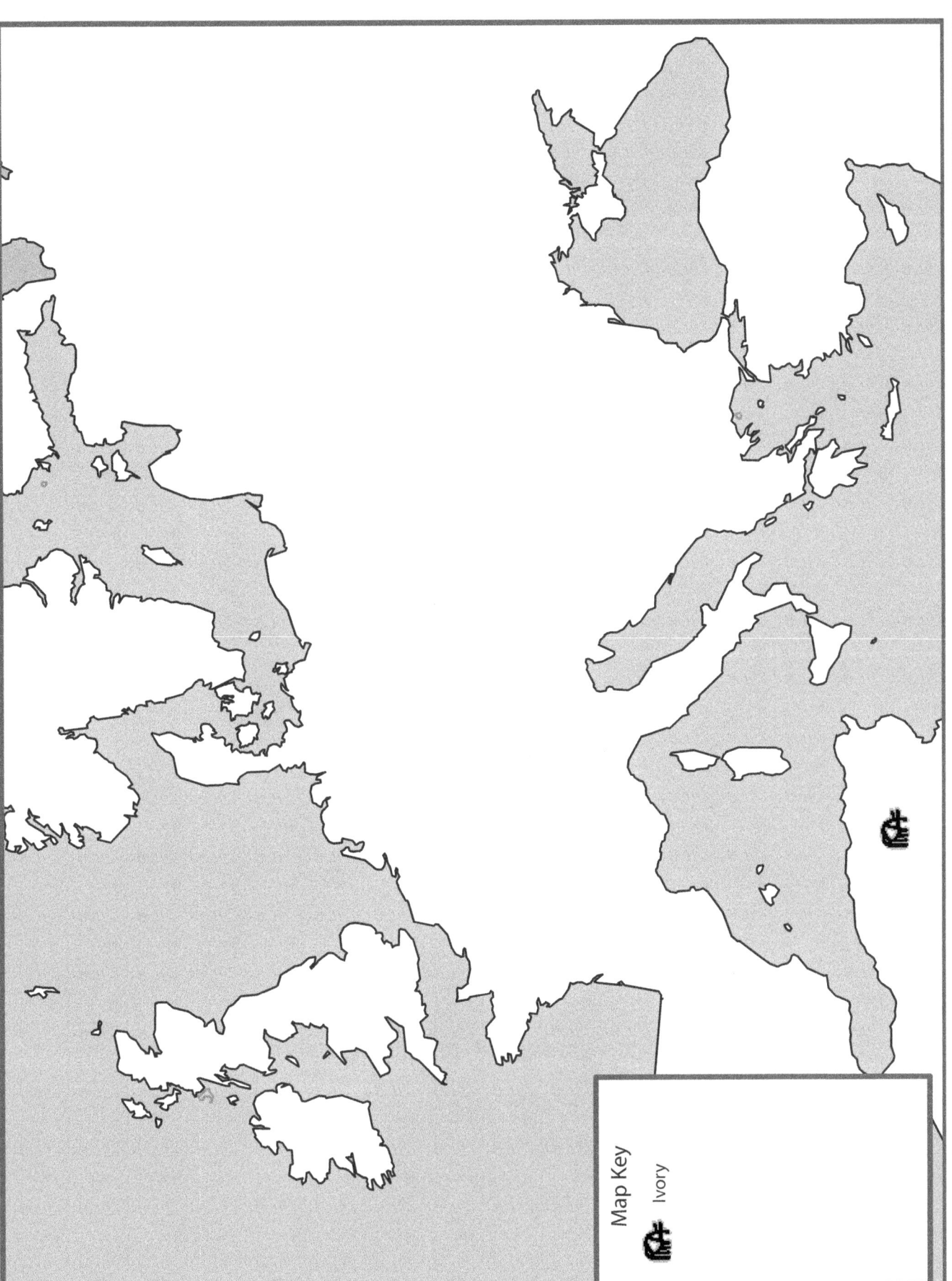

Map Key

✋ Ivory

History Odyssey: Middle Ages (Level 2)

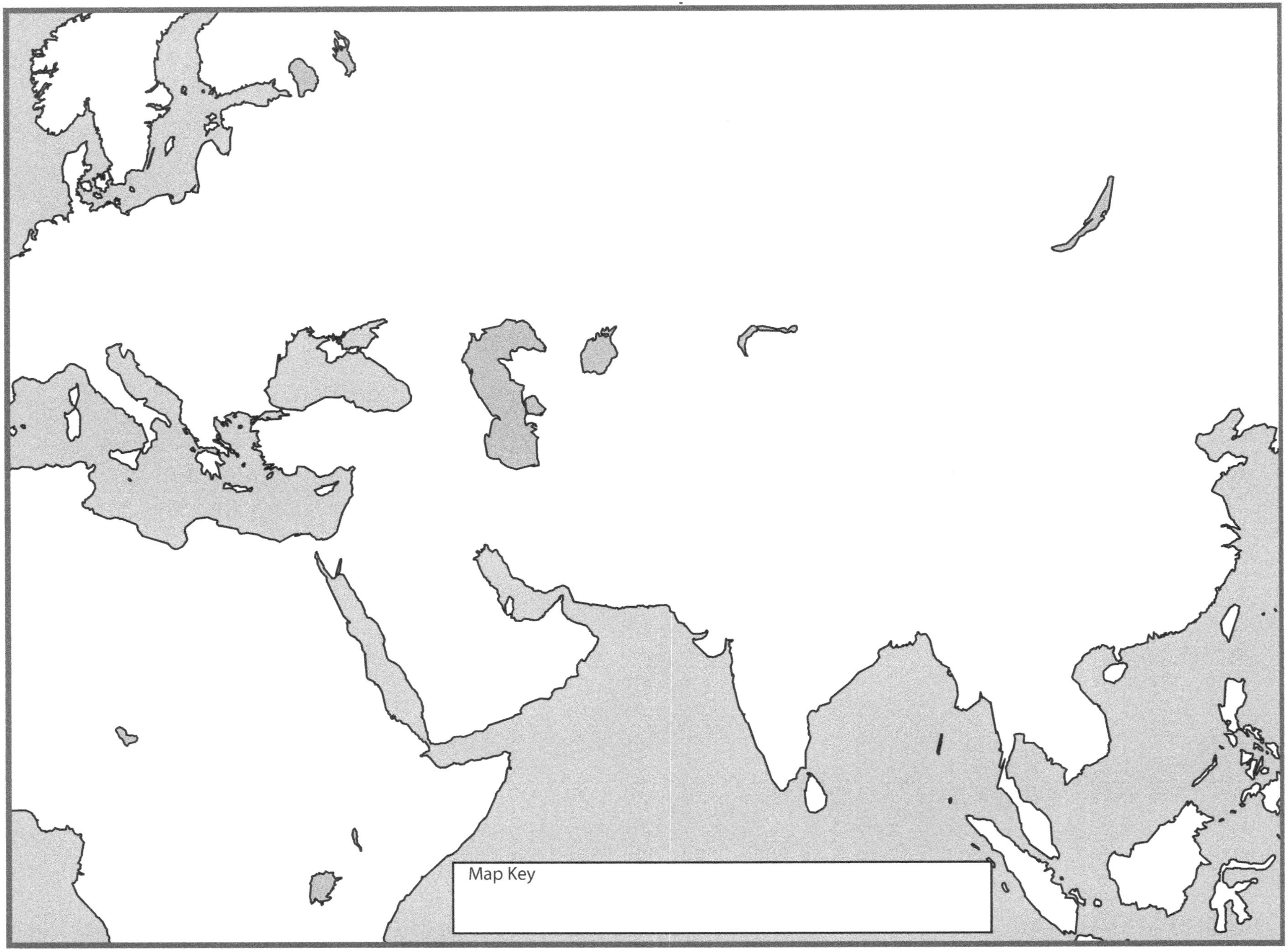

Medieval Explorers

Map 11

Map Key

History Odyssey: Middle Ages (Level 2)

Pandia Press ©2013

The Black Death

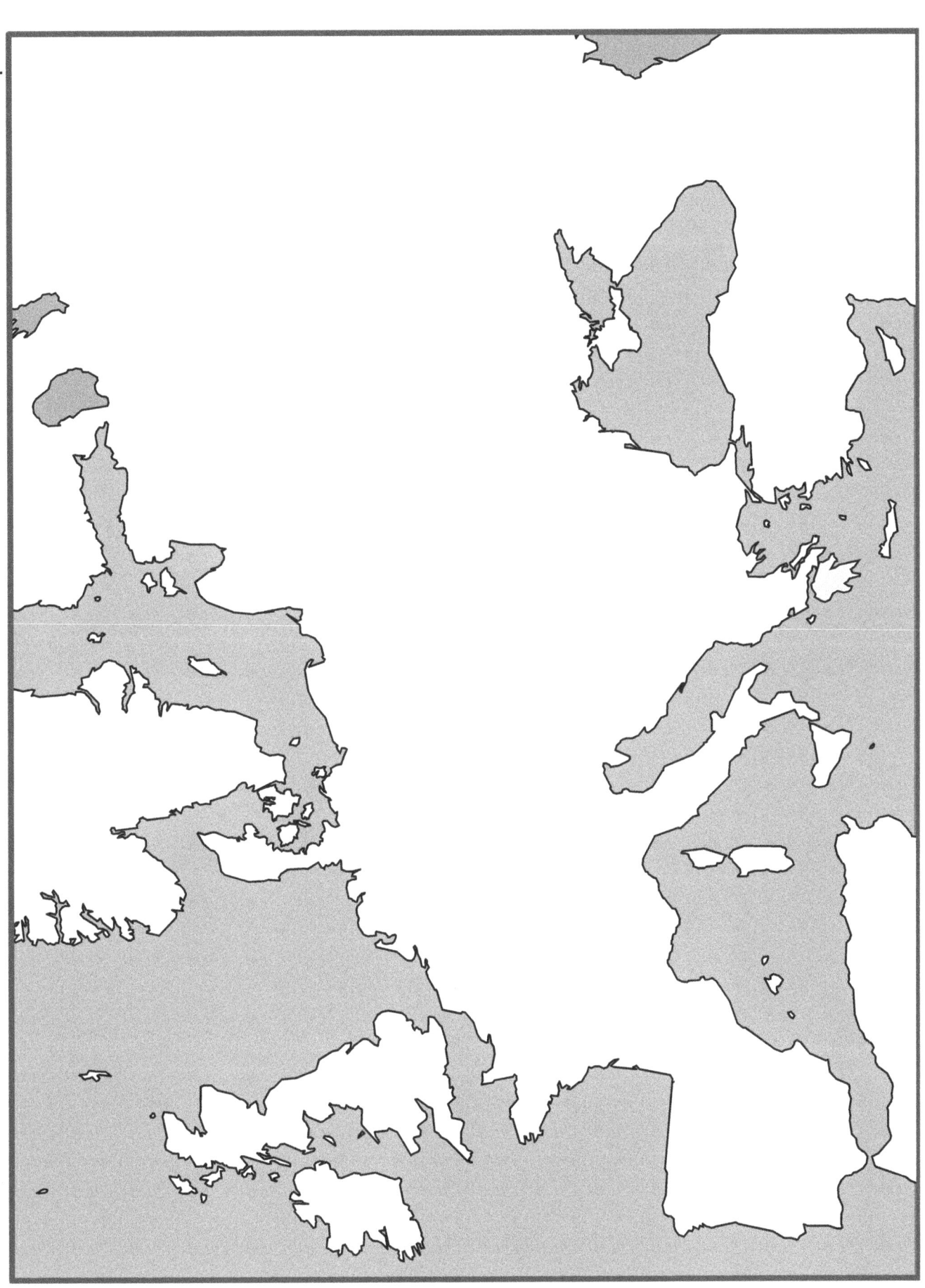

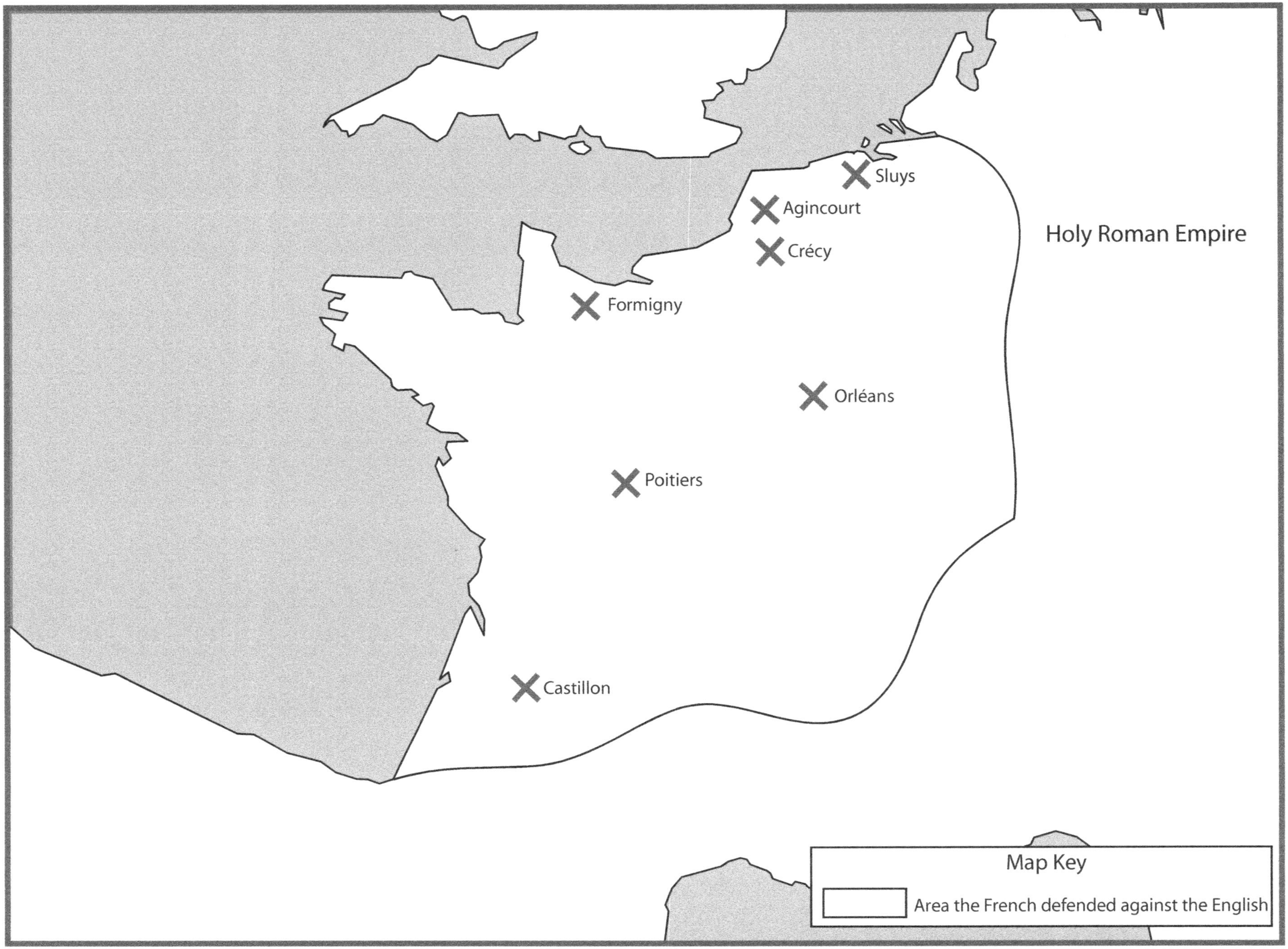

The Hundred Years War

Map 13

Holy Roman Empire

- ✗ Sluys
- ✗ Agincourt
- ✗ Crécy
- ✗ Orléans
- ✗ Formigny
- ✗ Poitiers
- ✗ Castillon

Map Key

☐ Area the French defended against the English

History Odyssey: Middle Ages (Level 2)

Pandia Press ©2013

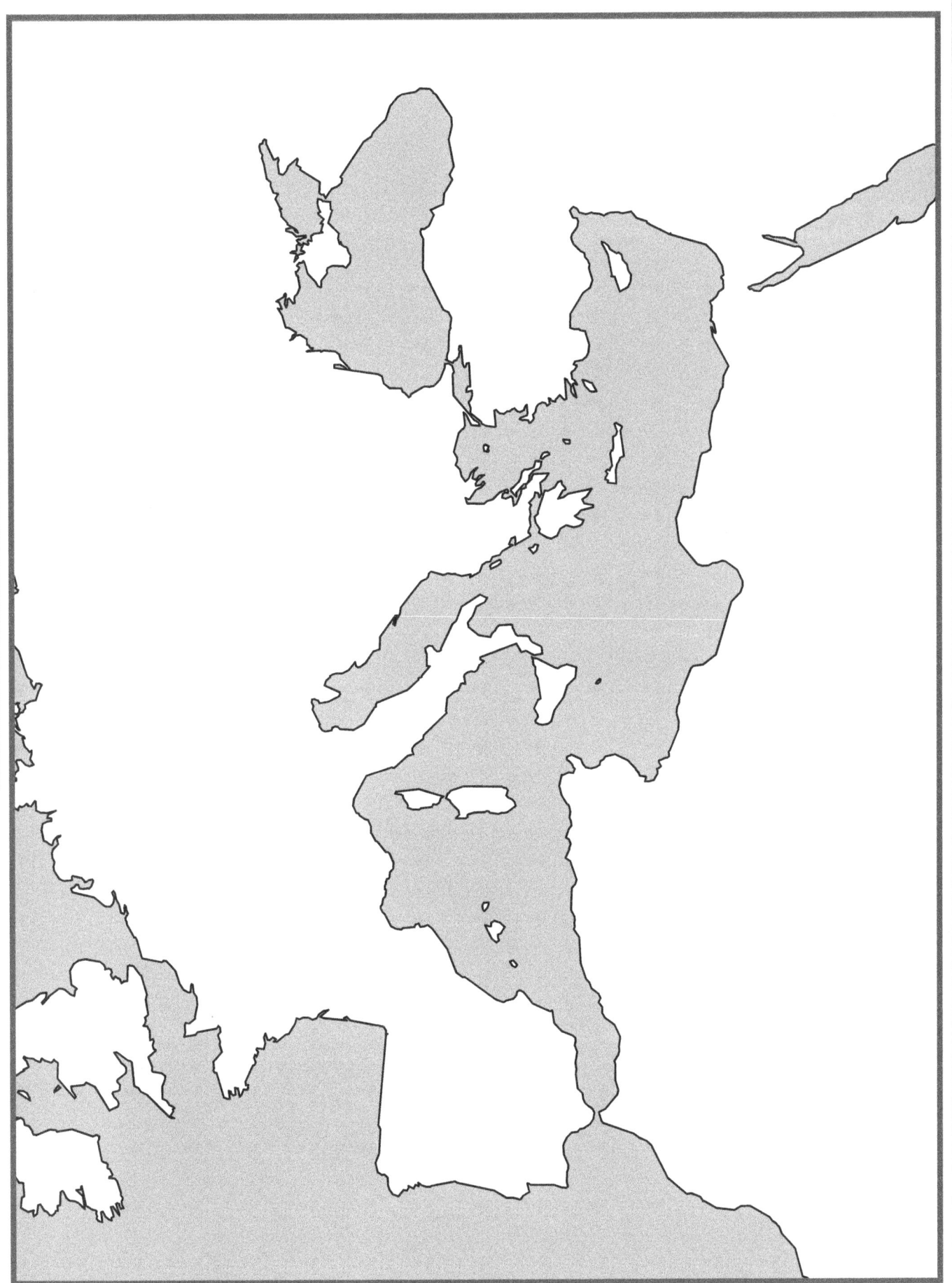

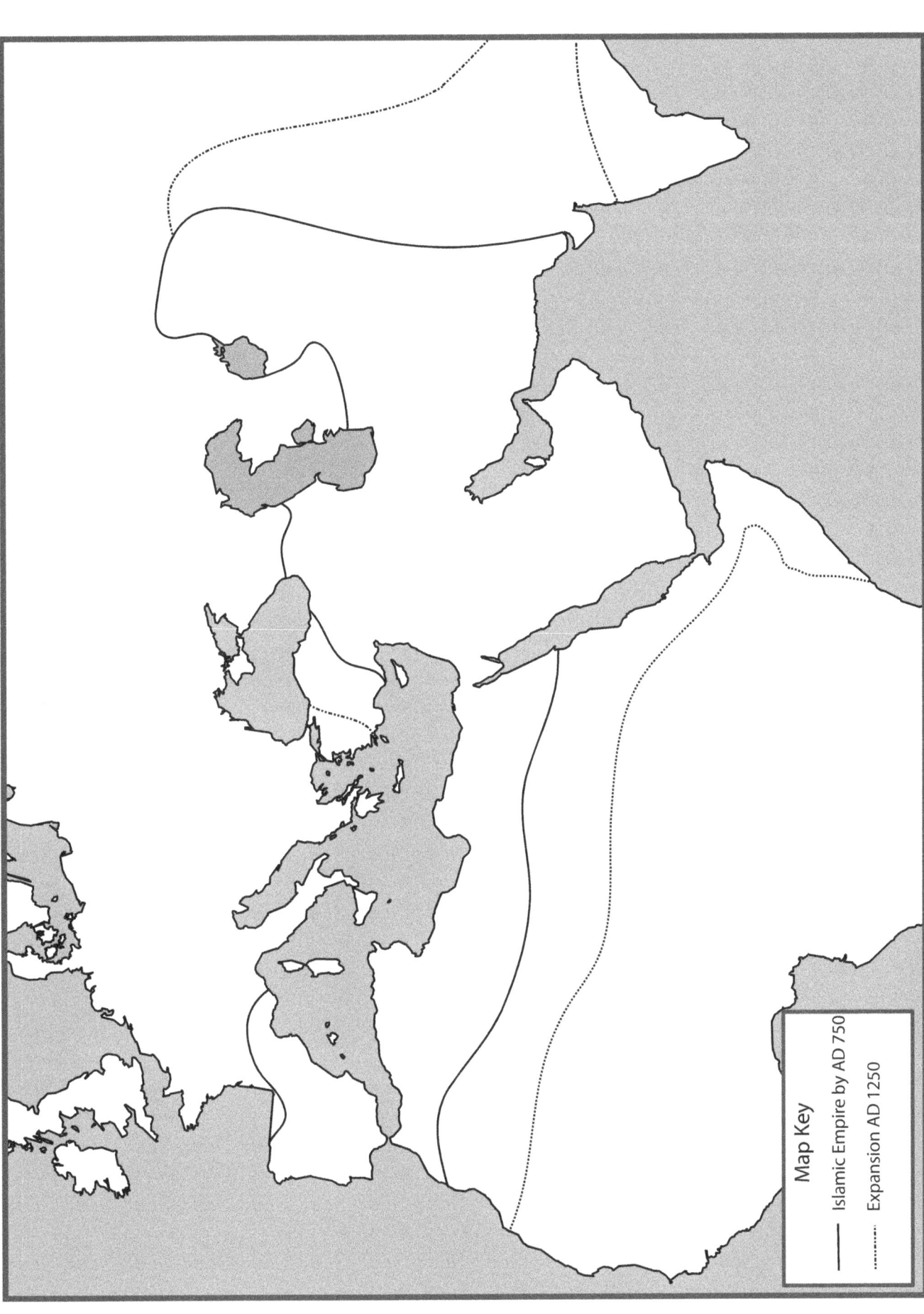

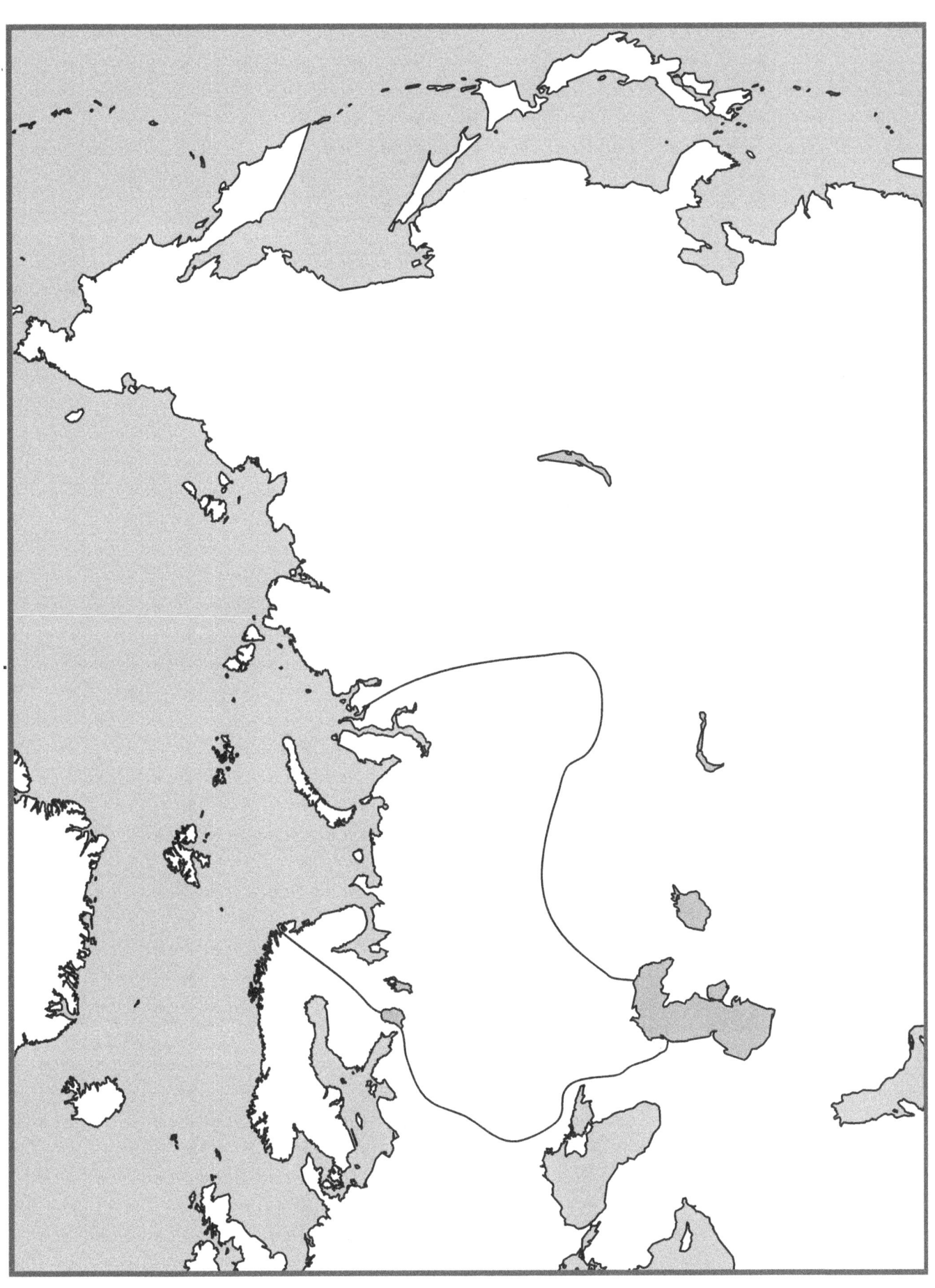

Map 17

Safavid Persia

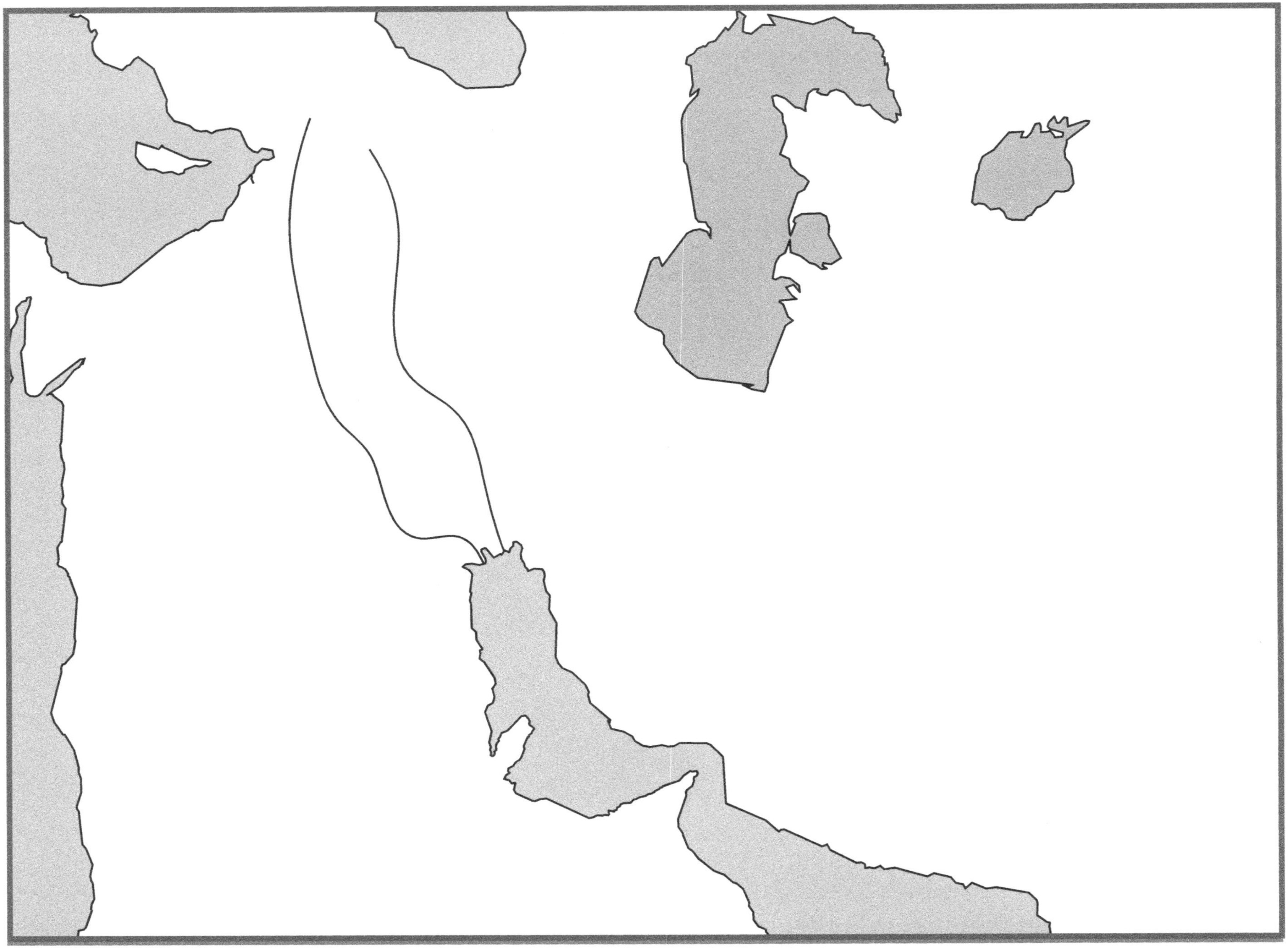

History Odyssey: Middle Ages (Level 2)

Pandia Press ©2013

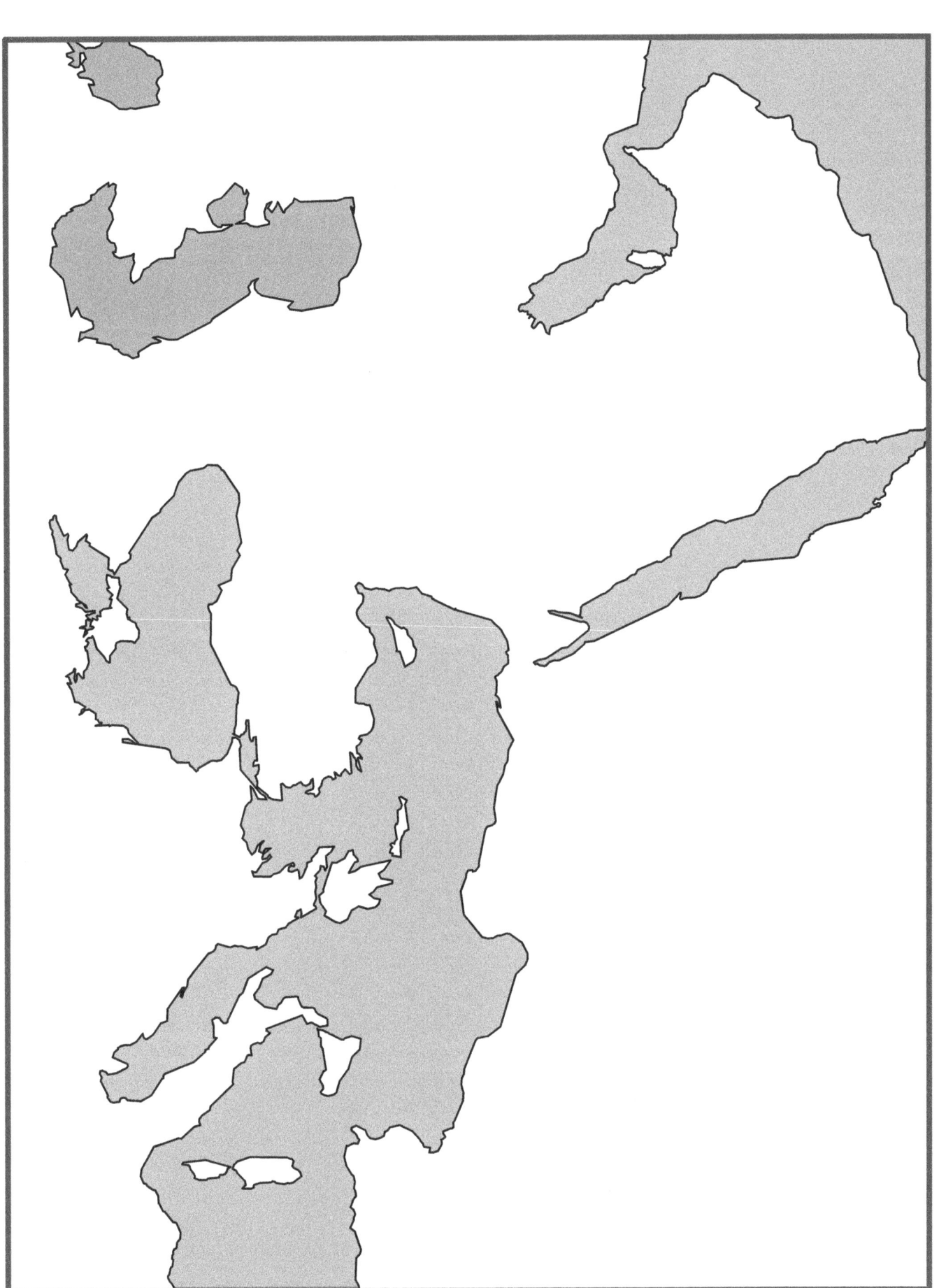

Medieval China

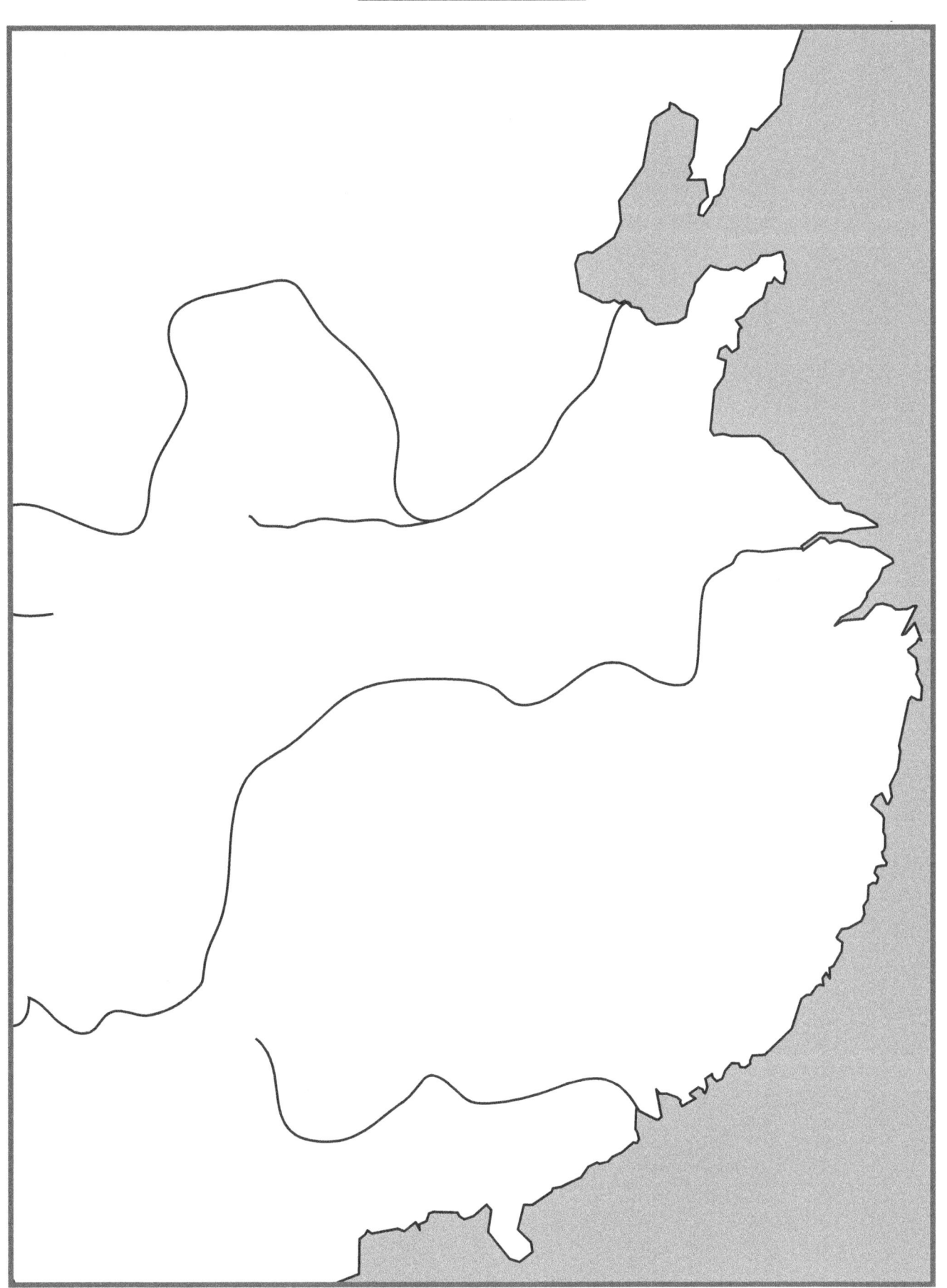

Map 20

The Mongol Empire

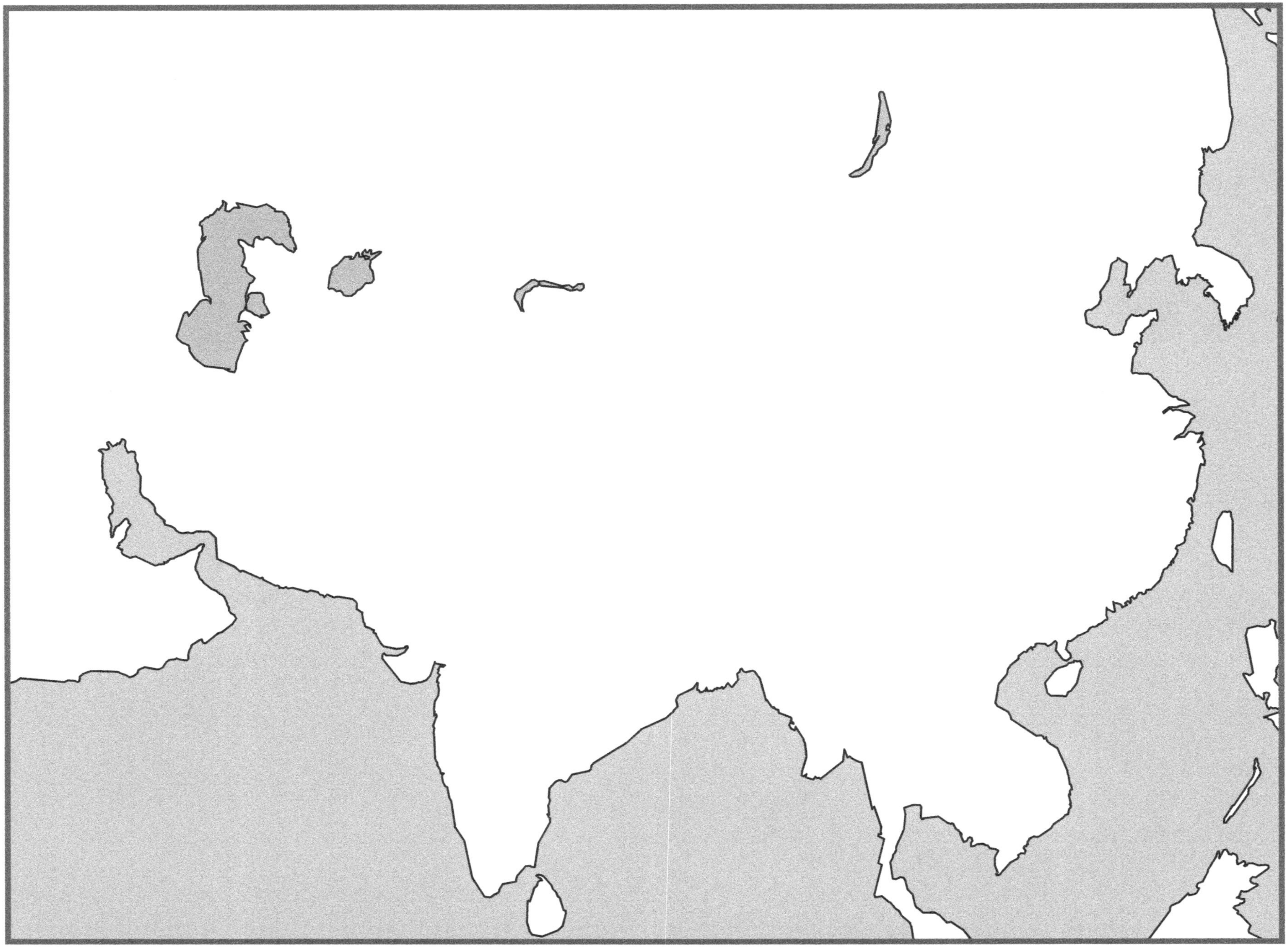

History Odyssey: Middle Ages (Level 2)

Pandia Press ©2013

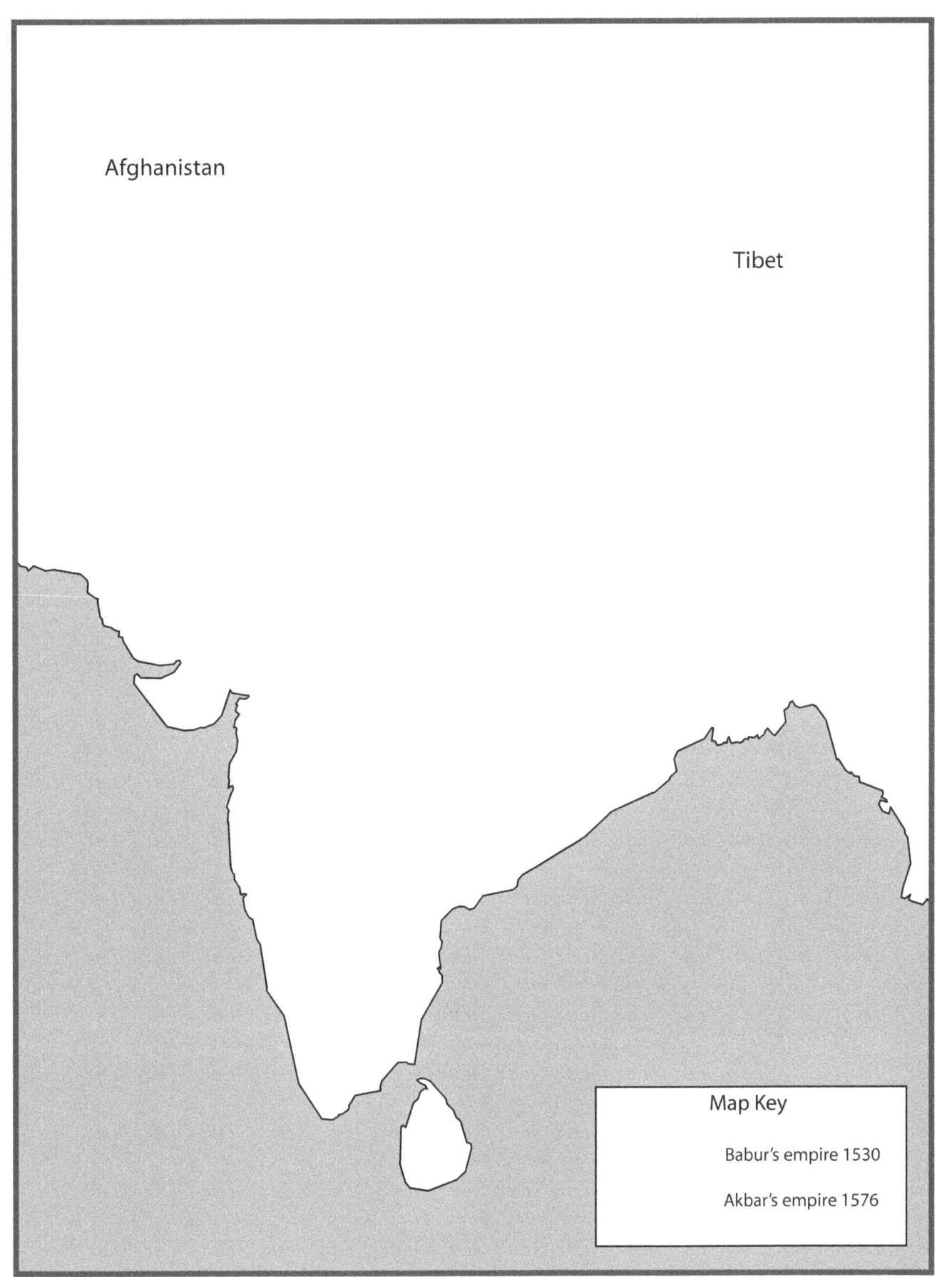

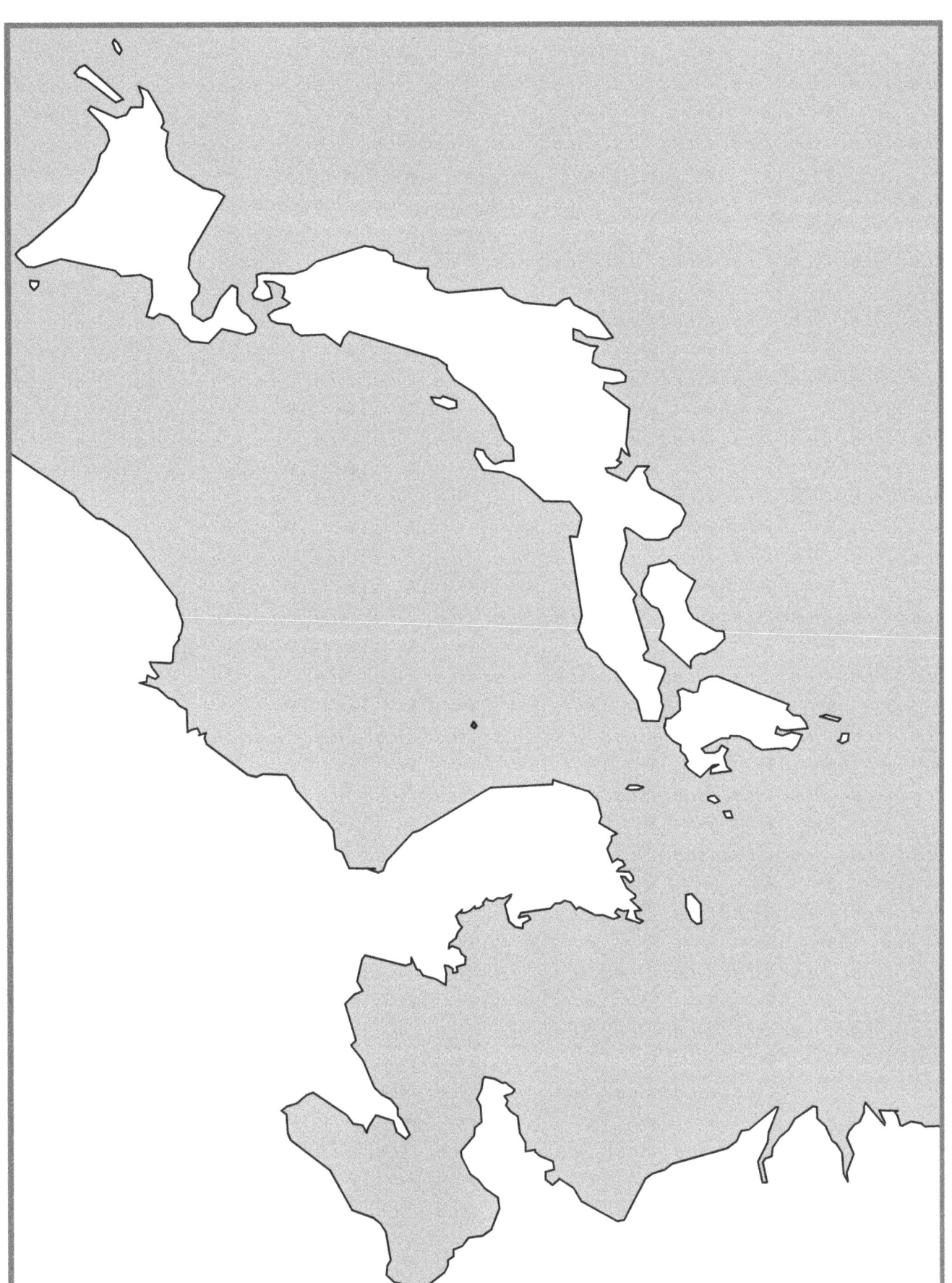

Medieval Japan

History Odyssey: Middle Ages (Level 2)

Pandia Press ©2013

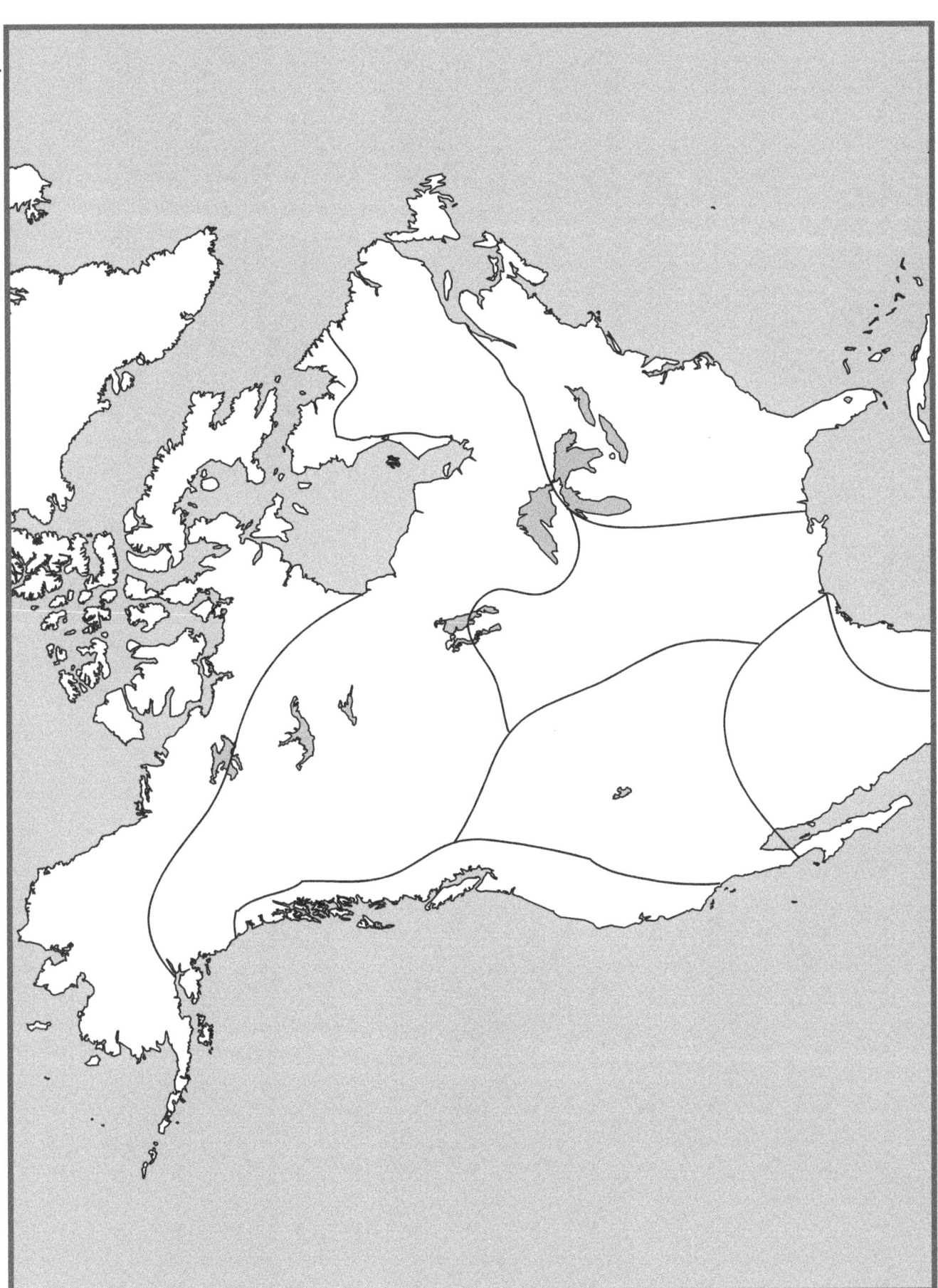

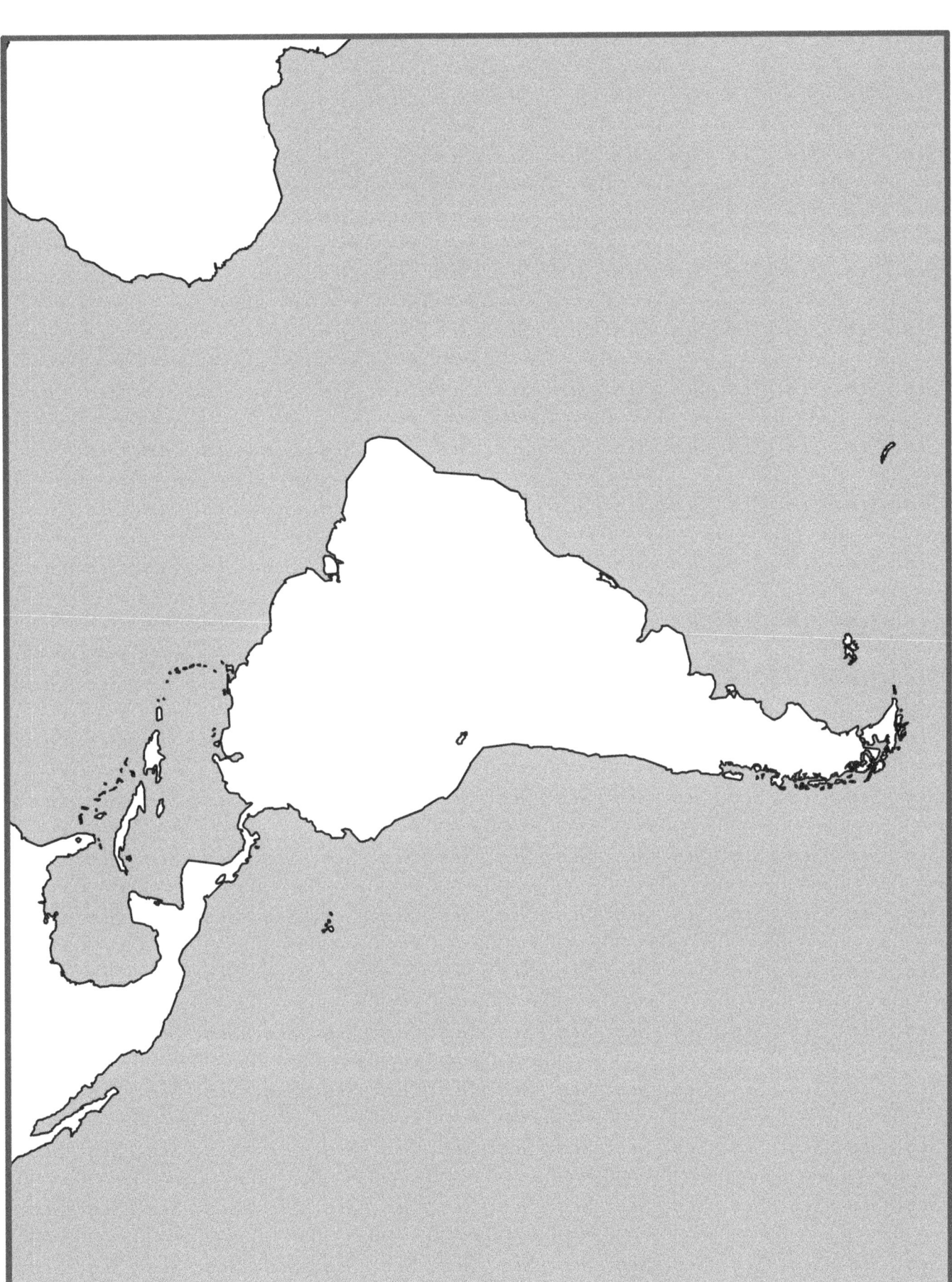

African Kingdoms

Map Key
- ☐ Ghana
- ☐ Mali
- ☐ Benin
- ☐ Great Zimbabwe
- ☐ Songhay

History Odyssey: Middle Ages (Level 2)

Pandia Press ©2013

The Reunification of Spain

History Odyssey: Middle Ages (Level 2)

Pandia Press ©2013

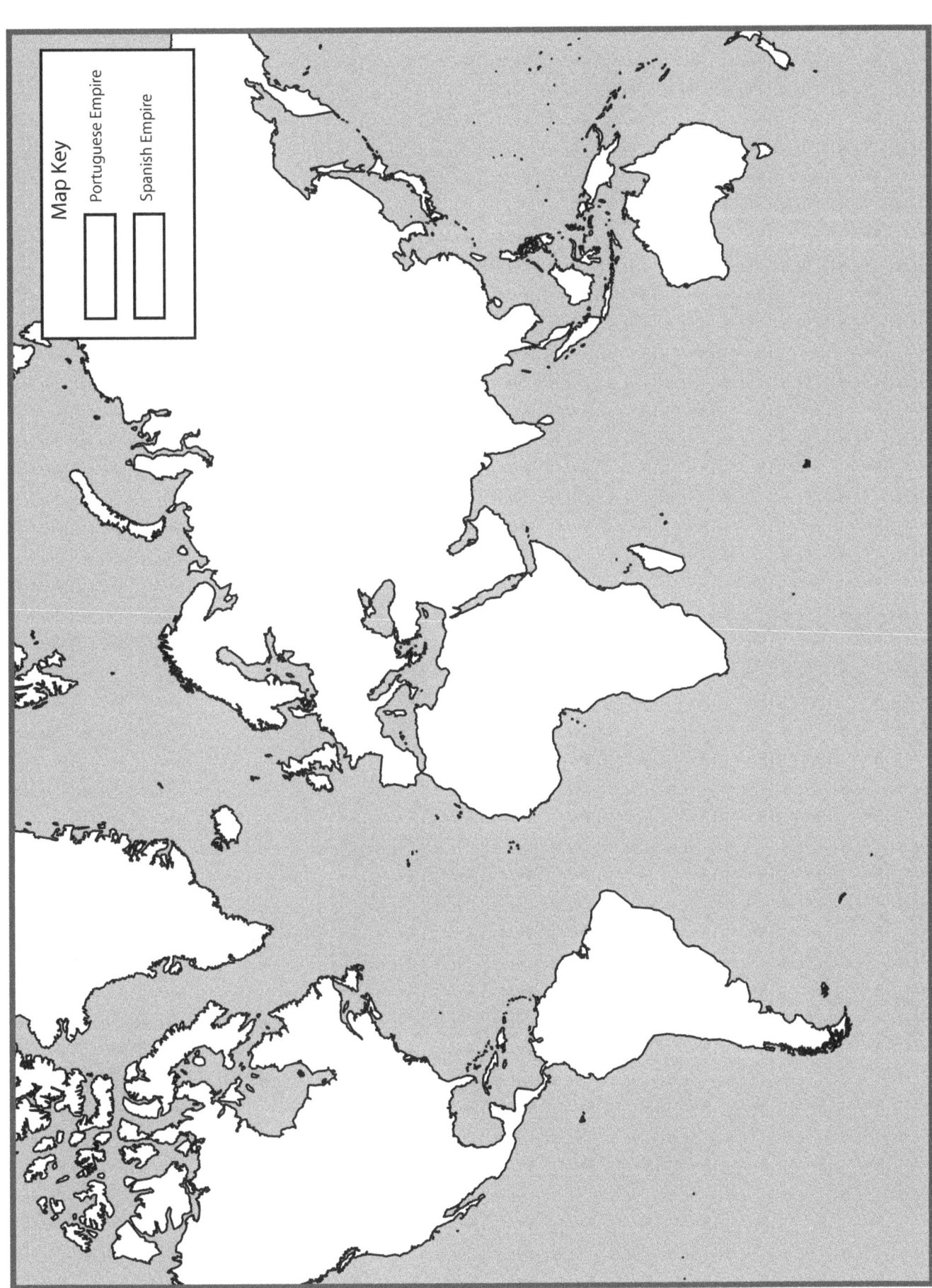

European Explorers

Map Key

History Odyssey: Middle Ages (Level 2)

Pandia Press ©2013

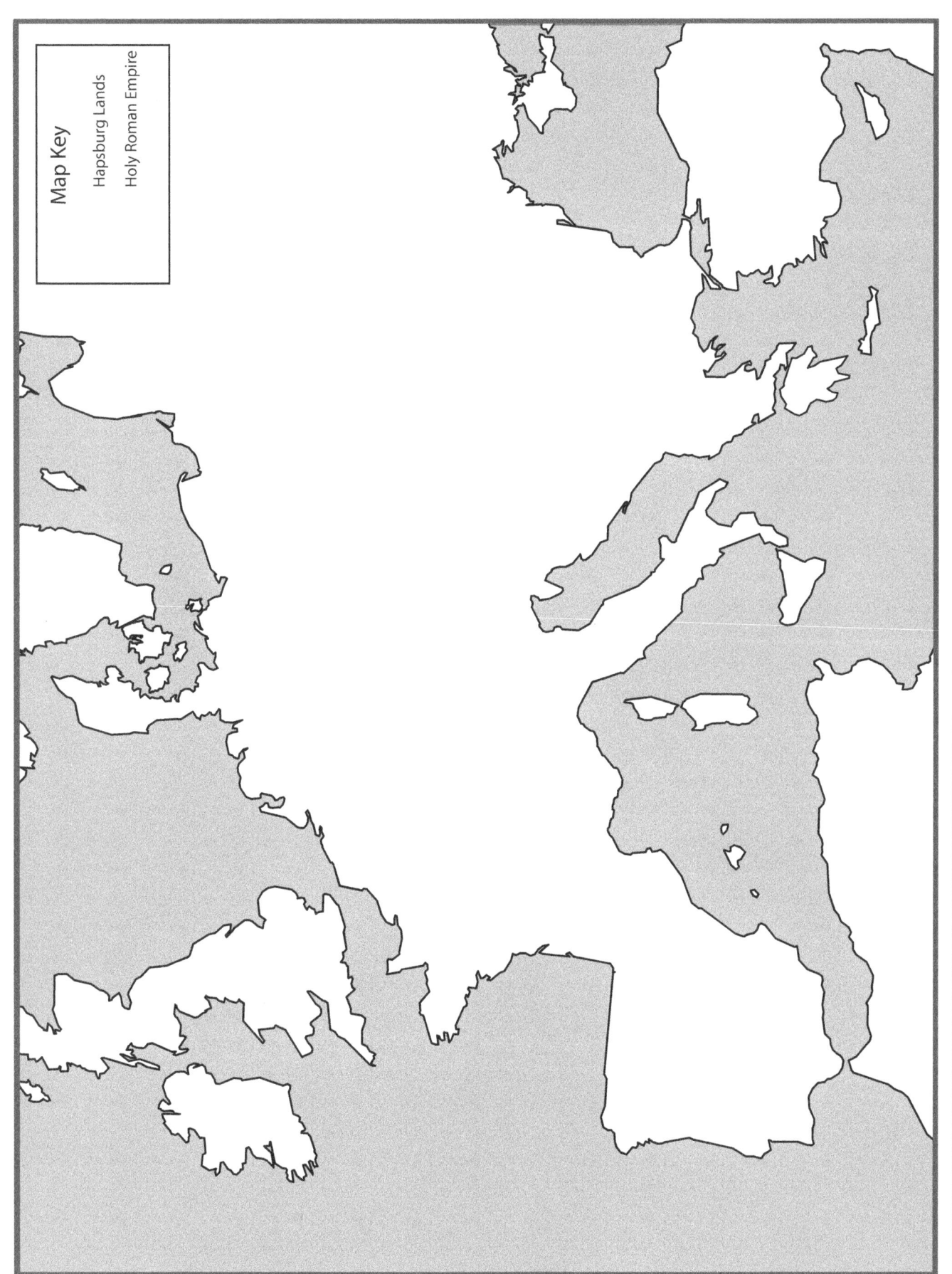